UNTANGLING
THE BUSINESS
OF DENTISTRY

UNTANGLING
THE BUSINESS
OF DENTISTRY

An insider's guide
to building a
thriving practice

By Doug Disraeli, DDS

Surrogate Press®

Published in the United States by
Surrogate Press®
an imprint of Faceted Press®
Surrogate Press, LLC
Park City, Utah
SurrogatePress.com

ISBN: 978-1-947459-67-0
Library of Congress Control Number: 2022912138

Book cover design by: Michelle Rayner, Cosmic Design
Interior design by: Katie Mullaly, Surrogate Press®

To my wife, Mindy, who has been my partner not only in life, but in all of my big dental decisions as well.

And to all the future dentists who will become better dentists from having learned from my mistakes.

Table of Contents

Preface and Introduction

When we were in dental school, we concentrated on the science and the technique. We learned a little about managing patients as we went through our clinics, and we learned how to be a community. What we didn't learn was how to run a business. There wasn't enough time and besides there was more interest in the need to pass the board exams.

Most new graduates became associates in an existing practice with hopes of one day owning their own business. Many of these associate jobs were with kind, older, experienced dentists who would introduce you to actual dentistry, warts and all. However, most dentists still wanted to be in control of their own dental lives.

This book is an "autobiography" with a goal to inspire and empower dentists (both new and experienced) to be proactive about business and marketing while providing a few tools and ideas on how to do so. There will be stories, pathways, formulas, and basic recipes that you can adapt to your own skills and needs. Success is really enjoying what you do.

I love what I do and what I do is dentistry. I love every aspect of it. If you haven't learned how to love it yet, you can. I want *you* to love what you do, be able to make a house payment, put money away for your children's education, pay off your loans, and even save some money for retirement. Dentistry has been very good to me, and I have made an excellent living from it. I feel I have helped a lot of people become less scared, be happier with their smiles, or even forget they ever had dental needs. I have had time to improve my skills and have had the audacity to be proud of them—well, at least some of them. I have had the luxury of making friendships with patients and peers. I have watched young patients grow up to become adults with good dental habits and I have watched adults grow older with a solid dental foundation to carry them through their golden years.

My practice has grown with the help of a lot of friends, peers, mentors, publications, seminars, and my caring staff. But there are many steps and plenty of time involved with expanding a practice. You have to pay attention to everything, which is a big commitment. At this point, I want to emphasize that every seminar you attend will give you a nugget of information, and it's up to you to listen. Read as many business publications as you can and talk frequently to your dental friends about business.

There are many reasons I decided to write this book. And let me caution you that it takes more than a weekend seminar to build a practice. There are a lot of small steps plus a few large ones, and I hope this book becomes a recipe for your success. Because this is a written manual, you can move at the speed and comfort that you choose. I originally thought this could be a manual for senior dental students and those newly graduated, but I realized this could be a refresher for any dentist who might feel their business isn't going the way they want. You will get more than one or two nuggets from this book, and it will help renew your love of dentistry.

My practice is successful. And, you may wonder, what the parameters of that success might be. For starters:

1. Our morning meetings are filled with energy and laughter.

2. Our days are filled with a schedule that is well balanced.

3. We all feel a sense of a job well done. We feel good about our ethical decisions.

4. We have the ability to do charity work and we do.

5. My team has full health insurance, bonuses, vacation and sick pay and a retirement plan that I supplement.

6. I am financially secure in a job I love.

Introduction: My First Office was a White Elephant

CHAPTER ONE

When I got out of dental school and went to work, I was so proud of my previous four years and couldn't wait to get to work every day. I anticipated talking about difficult cases, joking with my more amusing patients, and building rapport with my team. I was well trained and ready to go.

"Hey, check out those ninety-degree curves on the root tips! I can do this root canal." "Does anyone have any ideas on what to do with Mr. Grimace's cross bite?" "Wow, Mrs. Diamond wants a full mouth rehab. Let's get started"

The reality was a little different. I became an associate for a practice which had a 5,000-square-foot office with eight operatories, which was a little too voluminous. There were at least three dentists working at any one time. When I came on board there were four. Parking was a little sparse; we had four spaces, which were reserved for the dentists. Everyone else, including patients and staff, had to park on the street, which often meant parking up to several blocks away in a busy area. As I look back at the size of the office, I realize that we should have had fifteen or more operatories instead of eight—there was quite a bit of wasted space for the huge rent.

Our new patient influx rarely went over twenty patients a month total, which should have been the new patient flow per dentist. How did this operation make a profit? Once the curtain was rolled back, I could see that the profits were minimal. All the associate dentists were making less than a new elementary school teacher, but the promises of success never stopped.

I thought new patients were the key, so I did everything I knew to bring them in. I had business cards and passed them out everywhere. I joined organizations and bragged about being a dentist who would be happy to see new patients. I eagerly asked the few patients I did have, to refer their friends and families or even strangers they met on the street. The results were not impressive. I was not making enough money to see a future in dentistry. I got married two years after graduating and my wife started selling real estate and she was immediately able to start growing her business rapidly. In just a few months, she outpaced me financially.

"You're not doing quite as well as I had hoped you would be doing by this time," threatened Dr. Combover, the senior dentist.

"I'm having problems bringing new patients in," I said.

"Well, go get some! Be aggressive! Get out there!" he ordered.

"Would you be able to give me some advice?" I asked.

"Yes!" he said, with authority. " Work hard at it," Useless.

What went wrong? As I started looking at the business, I saw a lack of organization. The office's most long-term employee had only been there three years—there was a lot of turnover. No one felt appreciated and the dentists were frustrated. The owner's philosophy toward a dental practice was, "If you build it, they will come!" He invited dentists to come work for him, but expected them to build their own practice. He would provide the staff, the supplies, and the facility and pay each associate a fair percentage of their production. There were no contracts, just a handshake, which meant that things could change if he wished—and they often did. He didn't have a formula or data to support his ideas, he just thought they would work. The staffing had a high turnover because he expected them to know everything, but he never told them what he wanted.

"Oh my God!" I said to myself, "I'm so unhappy. I need to make a change."

I Have to Do Something!

CHAPTER TWO

I loved dentistry, but my desire was waning. It's hard to love something when you are not successful. You can only read so many journals and attend so many courses. As a result, my wife and I planned my escape from dentistry. I thought about going to medical school. This was before HMOs, when almost every doctor had a Mercedes and a mansion. But I didn't want to deal with death, so that was out. I thought about law school. I went to school with two friends that had gone to law school and were in similar points in their career. Although they were making a good living, they were both working a miserable sixty hours a week, so that was on a back burner. Really far back. I was making less than a teacher, so maybe I could become one and make more? Maybe I could go back to dental school and specialize.

The turning point came when I spoke to one of my classmates. Jake was one of my study buddies and I knew how good he was. He had gone to work for a dentist in Los Angeles, and he told really funny stories about the incompetence of the older dentist. But when Jake realized that the older dentist had a daughter in dental school, he knew his chances of staying in the practice after she graduated were limited.

Jake found a path out from under that funny, yet incompetent, dentist. He called me to brag about the new practice he bought. He had been in the new office for about three months and was having the time of his life. Couldn't I do that too? Wait a minute! If I buy a practice, then I buy the good faith of a lot of new patients at the same time. My earlier problem of getting only two to three patients a month would get an immediate boost.

I knew the answer in a millisecond, but I wanted to make sure I wasn't being stupid. I went home and talked it over with my wife. She agreed with me, and the next day I looked for a broker.

Connecting with a broker was easy. I called the local dental society and asked for a referral. Once I found a broker I was comfortable with, I told him I wanted to buy a practice. He answered questions I didn't even know I needed to ask. My wife was in real estate and was earning four to five times what I was making then. we were able to refinance our home in order to pay for the future new practice. The broker also let me know that there were banks that specialized in loans for the purchase of practices and it was a fairly easy process. Since my brilliant wife had set us up, all we needed was the refinance. The broker gave me a list of qualified offices and explained how it worked. The best part for me was that traditionally, the seller paid all fees. My only responsibility was the purchase cost.

I was able to do a drive-by, but I wasn't allowed to go inside during operating hours. The broker explained that there were many parts to the sale, and it all needed to be protected. For example, it is in the buying dentist's best interest to keep the existing staff. The transition would be a lot smoother with fewer changes and a working team is much better than dealing with a patchwork one. In some cases, if the employees know of a pending sale, many will start to look for a new job. The thinking is that their fate would be more of their choosing, rather than one being forced upon them. Will the new dentist be kind, skilled, generous, or not quite so much?

Another part would be to protect the patient base. If patients were of a pending sale, they might also think like the employees. Why not take this time to go to the dentist that our best friends recommended and is closer to home?

These concerns about employees and patients will still be there if you do a turnkey operation, in which the selling dentist hands over the keys on the close of escrow and bids you a good life. As part of the contract, the selling dentist will write an introductory letter praising the new dentist and encouraging the existing patients to "try him out." It's now up to the new dentist to do everything possible to keep the staff and patients. In a two-month escrow of purchasing a practice, if the staff and patients know it's happening in the beginning, the hill is steeper and longer to climb. By informing everyone after the sale, the employees get a chance to look the new dentist in the eyes and very often give him or her a chance. If they're on board, more patients will follow their lead.

I was able to go a slightly different path, and in my case it was worth it.

I looked at two promising offices only a few miles from where I worked. I didn't know how picky I would (or could) be, but those offices were dumps. I optimistically thought I could add the cost of decorating to my budget until I saw the financials. I learned that the usual purchase price was somewhere between sixty-five percent to ninety percent of the previous year's gross. One of the major factors to examine was the gross production and collection of the previous five years. One office had a steady decline of about ten to fifteen percent for four out of the five years. But the worst decline was about twenty-five percent on the most recent year. The asking price was eighty-five percent of the average of all those years. I didn't bite.

The other office was also declining, but not as fast. The real problem was the overhead. The rent, salaries, and dental supplies were way out of proportion. Average profitability runs about twenty-five to thirty-five percent. (There are general practice offices that are very efficient and get up to fifty percent, like specialty offices, but those are rare.) This office was around fifteen percent. I thought I could improve upon Dr. Sketchy's office, but not so sure I wanted to spend that much money in a gamble.

I ended up buying the practice of Gary, a dentist who wanted to become an endodontist and go back to school. He stayed with me for a year and introduced me to all his patients as they came in. He also wrote a wonderful letter and sent it out with an emphasis on the fact that he would be staying for a while before he went back to school. It was then up to me to "court" the employees and the staff. I sent a personal handwritten letter to every patient that came in, and I included something personal to let them know it wasn't a form letter.

Gary had a well-run practice and got me started learning about the business of dentistry, which coincided well with my knowledge of what I learned *not* to do. He was a great mentor who was very generous with his time and excellent advice. I was lucky. Gary was only a few years older than me and had a wonderful disposition. He was kind and had a face that smiled easily and often.

In my first month, I produced four times my best month working for the other dentist. The second and third months were even better. After my first year, I stopped looking over my shoulder. Within twenty-five years, I accumulated a lot of material from dental seminars, magazines, and peers. I started helping out less experienced dentists and formalized a study club devoted to the business aspect of dentistry. My thought was that dentistry had given me a great life, and I wanted to share my knowledge and experience with others.

What Do I Do First?

CHAPTER THREE

When starting out in the profession, the very first thing you need to do is remember that you are an ethical dentist, and you will continue to be one. The next thing is to always remember you are a business and every person you come in contact with can help you. This means you must always have marketing at the front of your mind, because public review websites are here to stay. Google and Yelp have a growing influence on your ability to attract new patients (and don't forget there are also many other ways to market your practice). When you consider that every action and communication will be judged mostly by a jury with a lower education than you, you will be more patient and kinder with your responses. Your ultimate goal is to increase your new patient flow and maintain the happiness of your existing patients. However, any misstep will be aired publicly. True, not everyone will have thin skin, and not everyone will jump on the internet for every slight transgression, but if you act as if they will, you won't have to worry.

On the other hand, being kind has its own rewards. When you call patients the night after treatment, or go slowly with an injection, or take extra special care with the color matching for an anterior filling, your patients will appreciate you. This appreciation comes in all forms, from a verbal thank you to tears of gratitude. Patients will bring you baked goods, arts and crafts, tickets to the theater, and so much more. Best of all, they will send new patients to you.

Rule one: Be a good, ethical dentist.

Rule two: Be a good businessperson.

Rule three: When in doubt, remember rule one.

There is an old saying, "Would you rather be happy, or right?" Followed closely by, "A happy spouse means a happy house." If we convert that to *dentalese*, "A patient to whom you are true will bring you a patient that is new." Basically, you should take the long-term view in every encounter you have with your existing or potential patients.

Gary, the dentist who sold his practice to me, stayed on for close to a year, working one to two days a week. His innate kindness was everywhere and was a great example to emulate. His professionalism was never in doubt when he met new people, but he made sure to recognize patients as people first.

One day during the first week I was there, Gary was standing outside of an operatory. He took a deep breath, let it out, then smiled and walked in. "Hi, my name is Gary. You must be Anne. It's genuinely nice to meet you!" he said clearly, with a smile and full eye contact. He then sat down and started a conversation about Anne's personal life by asking her questions. It seemed like he had all the time in the world. He actually only spent five minutes finding out about her life until he gently steered the conversation towards dentistry. He had his scheduler give him plenty of time for this important first visit. I had not seen anything like this before and it made a strong impression on me.

I asked Gary why he stood outside the operatory for a few moments before he walked in. "I got into the habit of stopping my mind from everything that had just happened before with the previous patient, so that it wouldn't spill onto the next patient. It allowed me to give all my attention to the patient that was in front of me." Needless to say, I started practicing this immediately.

Inadvertently, Gary showed me a path that was quite different than what I had been used to. In his world, Gary cared about his patients and wanted them to know it. Every interaction with every patient was an excuse for a positive connection. (He would have made an excellent politician.) This was the focus I needed. I didn't realize it, but I had arranged my dental life to be all things dental to all patients with an eye on making money, which is what my first employer espoused. Dr. Combover quoted the movie "Field of Dreams" often, "If you build it, they will come." Gary's twist to this quote was, "If you treat your patients with respect and care, they will trust you to do the dentistry that they need." This was a real "Aha!" moment for me.

Gary stressed quality and patient interaction. He didn't try to do twenty fillings and ten crowns every day with a few extractions and root canals thrown in (but if they were scheduled, he would be happy). His patients liked him, and they referred their friends, coworkers, and family. Gary later confessed to me that he was an introvert and eye contact was difficult at first, but he persevered and it finally became comfortable. He had gone to a seminar that gave him logical reasons to become more connected to his patients, and he found that not only did it work but he also enjoyed it.

I was very lucky to find a practice with a dentist that was so helpful. I have seen many that weren't, and in a few practices, the selling dentist had a hard time letting go. "Let the buyer beware," is an excellent warning. Is the office manager a spouse of the selling dentist and are they both planning on staying for a year or two? This can be tricky. Make sure that their final day is in the contract and only up to you if you wish to extend it. Make sure they understand that all new patients go to the buyer. Why would they want new patients if they are letting go of the practice? If they insist on which days they want to work and say that some new patients will prefer the old dentist, have a strong conversation with them on your expectations. You want a very cooperative selling dentist, and if they're not, don't buy the practice.

How Fast Can I Do an Exam?

CHAPTER FOUR

I quickly got into the habit of doing dentistry. We were busy, and other than trying to "be there" for my patients, I ran on autopilot. I had forgotten a lot of what Gary had shown me as it slowly became less important as I got busier. Unfortunately, that was a big mistake. I really didn't get into the habit of trying to improve my communication, marketing, or employee relations. I concentrated on doing better restorative dentistry. The rest could take care of itself. I was making money and I was happy…until one day I wasn't.

I received a handwritten letter from a new patient. He explained to me that my exam was one of the worst he had ever had. It was too quick and not at all informative. It was a huge mental slap, and it affected me tremendously. I remember doing the deep breath, big smile, and eye contact, and I felt like I was 'there" for him. He said that when I looked in his mouth, he wasn't sure if I had seen every tooth and every surface, or if I had checked his TMJ, or if I had done a cancer check or periodontal exam. He wasn't even sure if I had taken more than give a cursory glance at the x-rays. He wondered why he had to pay for it.

This was the beginning of my realization that running a practice wasn't going to be a shallow learning curve. There wasn't just one concept that would carry me through the end of my career. I had a huge mountain in front of me, but I felt like I was taking the first step. "Being there" for my patients was important, but so were a lot of other concepts—I needed to be open to innovative ideas and to challenge the status quo.

I was lucky because the man that wrote the complaint worked in marketing and wanted to see me succeed. He worked with me to develop an exam that I still use to this day. And unbelievably, he didn't charge me anything. He was in the beginning of his career, and he wanted referrals. But before I explain his method, I want to share with you an example of what not to do (and what I used to do).

"You need three crowns on your lower left teeth," said Dr. Overcharge smugly.

"How much will that set me back, doc?" asked Ryan.

"The financial secretary will go over that with you," Dr. Overcharge replied.

"C'mon doc. Give me a ballpark," coaxed Ryan.

"Well, it will be in the neighborhood of $6,000."

"Whoa, are trying to buy a new yacht? Are you sending your kids to a private school?"

"Uh, well, actually this is right in the middle of the average fees for this area," explained Dr. Overcharge.

"So, if I get this done in a blue-collar neighborhood, it'll be cheaper?" asked Ryan.

"I suppose that's possible," Dr. Overcharge replied reluctantly.

"Why don't you give me a twenty-five percent discount so that I'll get it done here, then?"

The marketing guy explained to me that **value** must be the first goal when sales are discussed, long before you discuss cost. If you create value, the cost becomes secondary. The more the patient feels the value, the less they are concerned about the cost. For needed dentistry, there is an easy formula. (This doesn't work for cosmetic dentistry, but we'll deal with that later.)

When you are ready to discuss your treatment plan with the patient, the very first thing you do is identify the problem.

"Mrs. Jones, you have a cavity in a tooth on the upper left. The cavity means that there are active bacteria eating away at your tooth."

"Mr. Gonzales, you have a cracked tooth on your lower right."

"Dr. Chan, you have an abscess at the tip of your upper front tooth, which was seen on the x-ray."

Once you have identified the problem, you explain what will happen if you do nothing. The deeper you go into the darkness, the better...within reason.

"Mrs. Jones, the bacteria will never stop. It will cause the cavity to get bigger and bigger over time. In the beginning, that growth is slow, but as the bacteria multiply, the cavity enlarges at a faster pace. If we do nothing, the decay will reach the nerve, and not only will you have pain, but you will also need a root canal, which is costly and time consuming. If we are unlucky, the bacteria will travel down the root, and we may have to extract the tooth."

"Mr. Gonzales, a cracked tooth only gets worse. The discomfort you are feeling now will only increase as the crack gets larger. It is quite common for the crack to enter the nerve, which not only hurts, but causes the need for a root canal as well, increasing the cost of treatment.

"Dr. Chan, the abscess is an indication that bacteria has entered the nerve. Since the infection is inside the tooth, your blood supply can't get to the source to destroy the bacteria, and the bacteria will continue to grow and thrive inside your tooth. The abscess will grow bigger and the expansion of the bone surrounding the abscess will cause a lot of pain. If left alone long enough, you will lose the tooth and lots of bone, and then it's likely the bacteria will travel to other parts of your body."

Once you have identified the problem and explained (in gruesome detail) what will happen if nothing is done, you can come in like the white knight with a solution.

"Mrs. Jones, your cavity is fairly small right now, so a filling would be an ideal solution. The smaller the filling, the more likely it will last a long time."

"Mr. Gonzales, we can place a crown over that tooth which will act like a band around a slatted barrel. Think of a wine cask with a metal strap. It will help hold the crack in place."

"Dr. Chan, in order to get rid of the abscess, we will need to clean the tooth from the inside out. The procedure is commonly called a root canal. We will clean out the bacteria, sterilize the canal, and then fill it back up with a material called gutta-percha which is a type of rubber. The gutta-percha only reaches from the tip of the tooth to the bone level. The rest will be filled with a tooth-colored filling."

NOTE, in this last example, I haven't discussed alternatives and what the advantages and disadvantages are. In order to be legal and ethical, you need to discuss these with your patients. So don't forget to do it!

Once you offer the needed dentistry, money is no longer the prime topic. It's involved but usually the first question from the patient is, "When can I come in?" or "How long can it wait?" You created value before the patient had monetary concerns. The money issues are still there, but not as pressing as the possibility of a root canal or losing the tooth.

In the example with Dr. Overcharge, he jumped right into the final solution, thinking that his charisma and experience would negate any objections. It was the equivalent of a physician saying surgery was needed without explaining why. Had he followed the necessary dialogue creating value, Ryan still may have objected to the cost, but he also might have tried to figure out how to afford it. To this day, I still occasionally find myself thinking I don't need to go through the steps, and it all comes crashing down when my scheduler tells me that the patient didn't make an appointment.

In every instance when the patient needs to spend money on treatment, this creation of value is necessary.

Okay, now that we have established the need for value, let's do an exam.

The Art of the Exam

CHAPTER FIVE

You can make a lot of mistakes and your office will recover. Make one in the exam and you won't recover, because this is usually the first time you meet a patient. This is where you get to show how thorough, professional, knowledgeable, and caring you are, without letting them see you trying to be. When you are done, you want your patient to look up at you and say, "WOW, that was the best exam I have ever had." And they will! This is also the first time your internal marketing will be based on your dentistry. Be prepared and have a plan…like this one.

Allow an hour for the exam and try to coordinate it with a prophylaxis afterwards. Sometimes the exam needs more time, but do not go over the time allotment because the patients' primary focus is usually getting a cleaning. If you reverse the order, the patient will often act jumpy and impatient to leave. If more than an hour is needed, tell the patient that "there are several options and I want to go over them myself before going over them with you." Tell the patient you want to memorize their case, thoroughly present it, and be able to give them the time they need for questions. Then ask to reschedule them for a week later, but make sure they realize there will be no charge for this next visit. There are a lot of dentists who schedule for a second visit routinely, and many consultants recommend this. But for most patients who come through as a new patient, this isn't necessary and it can be an inconvenience for the patient. How would you like it if you went in for a simple eye exam and the optometrist made you come back on a separate visit to discuss your need for glasses or contacts?

On the other hand, you also don't want to overwhelm your patient and then kick them out the door. So, every patient is scheduled the same, but at some time during the visit when you realize it's more complicated than what you can handle in a one-hour visit, begin to hint at a second visit.

The exam begins with the doctor walking in the room after the patient has been seated. You want to come in within two minutes after the patient entered the operatory. This shows them that you value their time. Walk into the far side of the room and turn around so you are facing them. With eye contact, a very confident voice, and a hand outstretched to shake, greet them saying hello and introduce yourself. Use your first and last name only and never include the title, "doctor." Even though it's a little less formal, you are setting the tone. The confidence with which you say your name slowly, clearly, and audibly is everything. Spend five seconds outside the operatory taking a deep breath so you can collect yourself and remind yourself to be confident (just like Gary).

After introducing yourself, sometimes the patients will introduce themselves as well and you'll get a clue as to what their preferred name is. If not, look them in the eye and say, "You must be Gladys Bigsmile," and wait for them to respond. Then ask them for their preferred name, make a slight show of writing it down, and then use it immediately to let them know you listened and made yourself comfortable with it. You need to use their name as often as possible without going overboard. Your goal is to make a patient for life, and you are making a connection every time you say their name.

Next, get some personal history. People like to talk about themselves when they realize someone is actively listening. Find out what they do for fun, marital status, children, pets, where they grew up, employment, and any other direction you are led. Ask follow-up questions like types of dogs or names and ages of their children. This is active listening, and it will go a long way. Find out enough about them so they can feel like you know them a little better than the last dentist. And here's the hardest part…write it down. It's okay to write it down in front of your patient, but if you have a good memory, write it down later. You'll probably remember most of it, but when you write it down in your patient's file, you'll have something to look at next year to remind you who this person is. When you ask about the prom their daughter went to last year, it's impressive. The more a patient tells you, the more they will feel connected to you. There is an area in your software in which to store this information easily.

Next, go through the documentation with them that they have filled out and pay attention to any dental discussion. There are three basic documents. The first is personal information, which includes the basics (name, address, phone numbers, place of employment and what they do, insurance information, referral source, next of kin, marital status, etc.). The second is the OSHA form, which needs to be signed. The last is a combination dental and medical history. All these forms are easy to get, and most dental software companies have them embedded in their program. I have added a few extra questions relating to aesthetics because I like to do cosmetic dentistry. I also ask about their previous dentist. Have there been any upsetting dental visits? Or an even better question might be, "What did your last dentist tell you?" Once you have the basics, you can tell if it's okay to ask more dental questions. Their forms will give you hints like, did the last dentist hurt them, ignore them, do unnecessary work, make them come back multiple times, or anything else you need to make sure not to repeat? When appropriate, always try to find out why they left the last dentist so you can avoid the same mistakes. If their reason for today's visit is cleaning and exam, still ask if there's anything they want you to pay special attention to. Ask cosmetic questions when you feel it's the right time, like, "If you had a magic wand, what would you change…about your teeth or smile?" The pause is sometimes seen by the patient as humorous and will hopefully amuse them, another positive thing. Note that the cosmetic question isn't a yes/no question, but rather one that requires some thought by the patient. This cosmetic conversation might be better saved for later in the exam. Play it by ear. Often the cosmetic issue is just planting seeds that may or may not grow.

X-rays are next. Make sure you know when the previous x-rays were taken before the patient has been seated (if possible). Insurance restrictions on x-ray frequency is a major factor, so this is important knowledge to have before requesting more. It would be very nice to have the previous dentist's x-rays, but it's not always possible. Always acknowledge the attempt to connect with the previous office. This will enhance the patient's belief that your office is proactive and will take care of even small issues. Take a very brief look inside your new patient's mouth, and then look them in the eye and say that you would like to take some x-rays. Have a hard and fast rule about x-rays, and then be prepared to bend. As you already know, patients have their own preferences and for different reasons, they often request no x-rays. Money, radiation, discomfort, and gagging all come into play, so be prepared to answer each one of the objections with a smile and confidence. There will be times where a previous dentist will be reluctant about sending x-rays. We all know that digital x-rays have a very low overhead, so if you feel you can't complete the exam without x-rays, it wouldn't bite too deeply into your bottom line to say, "Gladys, we have not yet received the x-rays from your previous dentist, but I can see questionable areas. Would you mind if I just took a few x-rays at no charge? Then we can do a better exam." Your assistant will be the one to take the x-rays, so reintroduce your assistant (who originally brought them to the operatory).

Intra-oral photos are next. Get an intra-oral camera, get used to it, and integrate it into your practice. A patient may not fully trust you when you describe a problem tooth, but when you show it on a monitor enlarged twenty times, it's hard to deny. Take a full-face shot. Take one of just the smile, then one with the teeth slightly apart to see incisal edges, and then one asking the patient to show as much gingiva as they can (this will help you later if you ever need to diagnose an anterior crown). Take a full arch of both upper and lower arches and then each individual tooth in numerical order (to help you label them later). If there is a perfect tooth, then take only one photo, but if there is anything going on, take multiple angles. Then take photos of any soft tissue abnormalities. You'll be able to see minor cracks in alloys, which we all know is a sign of probable decay. You'll be able to see clear cracks or lines that you can monitor later and compare. You'll be able to see bonding failures at their earliest signs. And you'll be able to see so much more. Best of all, you can show everything to the patient, who never fails to be impressed with your technology and your attention to detail. There probably won't be enough time to label them during this exam, but it is very important to label them as soon as possible (your assistant should be able to do this). Most dental software will allow you to bring up all photos and x-rays of a specific tooth at one time.

As a side note, you will see slightly disturbing things during the exam, but if you were being truly ethical, these are issues that don't really need treatment…yet. These are things like abfractions, clear enamel cracks with no symptoms, bulky margins, facets with somewhat rounded edges, etc. There are places in your software in which you can enter reminders to look at these specific areas during each exam; areas that you have suspicions about, but you are not sure enough to commit to a drill. Make sure you access these reminders every exam and let the patient know you are watching carefully. This is a very soft way to lock your patients into your office. They will wonder if the next dentist has this same information and whether or not they will be as conservative as you.

Many dentists want diagnostic models. Do them now.

After the assistant is finished with the x-rays and photos, the doctor is notified and spends a few minutes alone (away from the operatory) going over the results while the assistant puts things away. I say alone because then the patient doesn't have to watch you or judge how much time you spent going over results. When you are finished and have a few notes (if needed), go back in to the operatory with your assistant and say something to the patient that indicates you have already spent some time with the x-rays. "Wow, you're one of those people with very few restorations," or "It looks like someone in your dental history knew what they were doing." Then let them know that you are going to look at every tooth from every angle, and that your assistant will take notes. This is not the time for levity. Be serious. Gear up and begin the intra-oral exam.

Start on the upper right, "Tooth number one is missing," or "Tooth number one is fully impacted, fifty percent impacted," or "Tooth number one is okay," or "Tooth number one has an occlusal stain towards the distal. There is a buccal gingival decalcification and a wear facet on the mesio-buccal cusp." Use very detailed industry language. Your assistant doesn't need to write it down that way, but the patient needs to hear the familiarity you have with your field. Go through each tooth and make a comment about each one. In some cases where you know there is a problem, say, "Tell me about this tooth," or "What's going on with this tooth? Are you having any issues at all?" You are planting a seed that you will fertilize later in the exam. Several times during this exam, find some dentistry you can compliment and know that when you show the photos later, they can *see* what you mean. If your patients understand that you can recognize excellent dentistry, they will trust that you will do so for them. After you have mentioned all thirty-two teeth, it's time for the intra-oral cancer exam.

Tell your patient you are doing a cancer exam. For those of you that have technology, use it now. If not, then do it the way you learned in dental school but slowly and add some theater. Grab the tongue with some gauze and pull it out and to one side. If there is a short lingual frenum, tell the assistant to write it down and then tell the patient what that means (basically that they are handicapped when sticking their tongue out) and tell them you will avoid dragging it across their lower teeth. Mention *everything* you see (varicosities, enlarged papillae, slightly swollen Wharton's ducts, etc.), and write it down. Then palpate the sublingual glands with a finger inside the mouth and fingers on the outside of the mouth pumping back and forth to see if it feels normal. If it is, tell the assistant to write it down. If it isn't, make a note and go back to it later. Put your index finger on the buccal of #17 and slowly slide it along the attached gingiva all the way across to #32. You are palpating for swelling, easy bleeding, exostosis, etc. Repeat this on the maxillary teeth. Then gently pinch the far side of the corner of the lips (where upper and lower lips meet) and gently roll/massage the lower lip between your thumb and forefinger as you move your fingers towards you and when you get to the nearest angle, slide to the upper lip, and end up where you started. And don't forget to tell your assistant all your findings.

Put your index fingers in the cheeks along both sides and pull the cheeks out as you have the patient bite down so you can see the buccal view unimpeded. Again, mention everything. "The attached gingiva appears to have proper thickness. There is a little recession on #24." Mention crossbites, abrasions, and anything else you see. The more you talk about them, the more impressed your patient will be.

Once you are done with the intra-oral exam, it's time to check the TMJ and lymph nodes. Consider taking your gloves off since they are wet with saliva. You don't have to replace them, but if you feel more comfortable being gloved you must change gloves (this has probably changed once the COVID-19 protocols were put in place). Ask the patient if there are any issues with the jaw joints and listen to the answer. Make sure your assistant writes it down. If your patient wrote something in their history, ask about it again now. Then put your fingertips on the joint and ask the patient to open and close slowly. Mention crepitus, slight side shift upon opening, non-reciprocal upon closing, early opening click before translation or at dislocation. You get the idea.

Then do the medical doctor thing and check the lymph nodes at the front and side of the neck. If you feel something but very minor, it is a slight bilateral lymphadenopathy. If it is uneven you need to make sure the patient is aware of this and should see a physician, unless they tell you of a one-sided infection/inflammation in the recent past. If they are overly large, the same thing applies.

You can either do the probe yourself or let the hygienist do the probing (I usually defer to the RDH).

The exam is now done, and it's time to go over the findings.

If there is a lot of dentistry needed, you would have already started the preparation for a second visit. But for every patient, bring up the photos on the monitor in front of them and go through the photos. Make sure to mention the normal anatomy as a baseline so that the patient is educated, and definitely stress the excellent dentistry when seen. Point out the areas that are not normal and when they need treatment. Start to plant the seeds. For those areas that are not normal but need no treatment, say that we will keep an eye on this, and that it will be nice to be able to compare these photos against any future changes. It's now time to create value as discussed in the previous chapter.

For the problem areas, make sure to clearly identify the issues. After the description is complete, go into a detailed future if nothing is done to fix the problem. Don't offer a solution…yet. All the problems need to be presented before going into options. Remember not to skip this part as it is critical in getting the patient to do necessary treatment.

For those patients with only a few teeth that need treatment, describe options after the photo tour. Go through risks, benefits, and alternatives as a general background, and then get specific for each tooth or area. For the more involved treatment plan, reschedule.

Make sure to leave enough time for questions. If there is minimal time, then begin the process of rescheduling to make sure the patient does not feel rushed. But for the most part, an hour is plenty of time for the patient that needs just a few restorations. If the patient is not getting a prophylaxis, it's time for the handoff. If there is going to be a prophy, the handoff includes an introduction and interesting information about the patient to the hygienist. If you think a second prophy or a deep cleaning is in order, plant the seed now. If you warn the patient that they might need a second cleaning, they won't be upset if they need one, but if they are told after the prophy, it looks bad.

Ask the patient if there are any dental questions. After answering everything, walk the patient to your financial coordinator if there is no post-exam prophy scheduled. If there is a prophy scheduled, your hygienist will do the handoff. The details of a superb handoff will be discussed later. If the patient has not yet met the financial coordinator, make sure the introduction is clear and not rushed. Also mention that she or he will be answering all of their non-dental questions including timing, costs, and insurance, adding, "But please ask Penny to contact me if there are any other dental questions that arise." When you have completed the handoff, make sure you say goodbye with eye contact and mention what a pleasure it was meeting them.

Phew, that's a lot for you to handle. You may need to incorporate this a little at a time with your staff, but if you follow this you can make mistakes elsewhere and still retain this patient. Practice all this until it becomes second nature.

My Front Office Did What?

CHAPTER SIX

Okay, I now understood the new patient exam. The marketing guy threw me into the middle of a tornado, but he also pulled me out with a better grasp of the process. I still had a lot more to discover and quite a few more challenges to encounter.

Little did I know that the next challenge was a lot sooner than I expected. My front office manager was pregnant and announced she was leaving to become a full-time mom. "Wait, I'm not ready for that," I yelled at the walls. I had to find someone new.

This was back in the dark ages before the internet. There was a "Jobs" section in the classifieds of the local newspaper. Sometimes you really don't know what you don't know. I didn't know how to write a help-wanted ad. I didn't know that there was a wrong way to do it, but I found out quickly. After I placed my ad in the paper, I received over a hundred resumes from prospects through the mail. I had to sift through all of them looking for the ideal person, the ideal fit. I had no idea what the ideal fit looked like. I was young and I thought a young person would blend in well with my office, so I thinned out the pile getting rid of those older "set-in-their-ways" type applicants. By the way, hiring for age is discriminatory, but I didn't know that then. I ended up interviewing about five women and hired one who I thought was the nicest.

The person I hired had no dental experience. She was very nice, very polite, and very out of her league. I couldn't train her because I was too busy and there was no one else who could spend time with her. I tried teaching her dentistry after work but realized the mountain was too high. I let her go. I wasn't stupid—just ignorant. I asked Gary what to do. He had me write a list of the things I wanted in my new employee. I showed him things like nice, polite, had good grammar, and was presentable.

He laughed at me. "Don't you want her to know how to schedule a root canal next to a crown delivery?"

"Oh," I said sheepishly. I then wrote out a list of everything I thought I would ever need, but I kept nice and presentable on there, too. It went on for about ten pages. Gary looked at the list.

"Does this mean if any one thing is missing on the list, they'll be disqualified?"

"Uh…of course not," I stammered, when I really meant yes.

I wrote a new ad and included phrases like "Happy office looking for…" and "Be a part of our team…" and "Proper grammar is important." Well, actually I didn't add that last one. But this time I also added, "Five years dental experience required." I received about ten legitimate resumes.

Gary was at the office on the day that I scheduled the first interview, and I asked him to sit in. It was the marketing guy all over again. After the first interview, Gary asked me if I had ever interviewed anyone before.

I replied that I had, but that I never had training in it. He said I spoke more than I listened and basically the interview was all about me trying to get the applicant to work for me. I might get lucky and hire someone wonderful, but it was more likely I wouldn't. Gary and I worked on an interview questionnaire that I have refined over the years.

It's never easy to interview. When there are several good choices, how do you choose the right one? And when there are few choices, do you *have* to pick one? You might get lucky and the right person will convince you to hire him or her, but that's not likely. The interview process in the next chapter will help you narrow the field.

How to Interview

CHAPTER SEVEN

Before you get started on the interview, you should have a resume from your prospective employee to give you some guidance. There are real guidelines on how to write a resume properly, but most of the people you interview won't even be close. Allow some leeway if you can see the effort, but use your judgement if it's a little sketchy.

I look for a few things. The first thing I like to see is a long-term relationship with a former employer. You may have someone who bounced around in the beginning of their career but finished strong with a five-year employment with one dentist. It shows that they can get along with someone for an extended period. In the beginning, they may have had bad luck and chose a job that did not suit them, so they left and found one that fit them better. Sometimes it's not the employee but the employer. I know a lot of offices that promise roses and raises but end up giving thorns and threats. (During the interview ask about all former employers. And then ask why they left.)

Another thing I look for is gaps in employment. Unless there is an easy explanation, consider it a red flag.

It is worth your time to check each former employer. Call every one of them and really try to talk with the dentist. You are legally only allowed to ask specific questions, and the former employer should only answer the questions you ask. These questions are: "Did Suzie Suave work for you? When did she work for you?" And I always throw in a question that I make sound more legal than it is: "Would you rehire Suzie if she applied?" Check with your attorney to see if that will put you in legal jeopardy. (Employment practices liability insurance ((EPLI)) will provide coverage for claims made by employees alleging discrimination based on sex, race, age, disability, wrongful termination, harassment, and other employment-related issues.) What you are trying to hear is the inflection in the previous employer's voice. You can tell if the prospect was well liked or the exact opposite by the way the answers are given. And very often, if the employee was well liked, the former employer will go off script and sing his or her praises.

"Suzie Suave worked for me two years ago for about three months," said the former employer. "She was a dental assistant."

"Is there anything else you'd like to add?" asks the prospective new employer.

"No."

In this case, the former employer either got up on the wrong side of the bed, was a thorns and threats type of dentist, or he really didn't like the former employee. All of this would be useful information. Don't forget that one person's bad employee can be your excellent one. I hired someone who's resume was written horribly and didn't give dates on any of her former employers. When I called one of her former employers, I got the answer that made her sound like she was a bad bet. When I asked her about this in the interview, she was very professional and said it wasn't the right fit. Her interview went extremely well, and she has been one of my best employees of all time. (She told me later about her old boss. He was having an affair with one of the employees and tried to keep it hidden.)

Okay, now for the interview. These questions are the ones I use for every position in the office, and you can tailor them for your own staff. One of the main reasons for a face-to-face interview is to see if a conversation is comfortable or stilted. Can you see yourself working with this person? Make sure the interview is long enough to show respect for the process and to give yourself a chance to see past the surface. Sometimes it's difficult to continue when you know within just a few minutes that the candidate isn't suited for your office. However, give yourself a chance to overrule your first impression as well as show respect to the applicant by being serious about the interview.

While you are conducting the interview, take notes and refer to them later in the interview. It shows respect and that you are listening. These interview questions are an accumulation of many years of trial and error. Whenever I could, I would ask my colleagues what questions they ask during an interview. I went to many seminars and when they discussed the interview, I took notes. Sometimes I ask every question but most times it feels right to skip some.

Here are some things to consider when interviewing for staff members:

1. Ask non-resume questions. "Tell me about yourself. Things that aren't on your resumé." You have already asked this question, lightly in the phone interview, so to not look stupid, write down the answers given over the phone. I would repeat the "not on your resumé" phrase to encourage them to discuss hobbies, talents, and family interests. If they don't want to discuss anything else, that's fine. It's not a negative, and besides, it's against the law to ask why they have nothing to add. That's why I simply leave it at, "Is there anything you would like to add?" I like knowing about spouses and children and hearing how they talk about their families, but once again, keep it legal. If you stay encouraging, your interviewee should be a bit more comfortable talking to you, and the rest of the interview should become more relaxed as well. This information can also be useful later in the interview if things are going well and you want this person to work for you. It will help you make a connection.

2. Focus on what they do best: "What are your strengths?" This is a common question, and I really don't like it, but you need to ask it. Most of the answers are as predictable as a Ferris wheel. Occasionally you'll hear a really good answer. If the prospect hems and haws, they weren't prepared for this very obvious question. Did they think they were so strong of a prospect that preparation was beneath them? Common answers include comments about working well with others and being a self-starter. In my opinion, that's a very neutral answer...and safe.

3. Ask about where they could improve: "What do you consider to be your weaknesses?" This is also a horrible question, and I hate the answer you almost always get: "I care too much." But it is extraordinary how often an applicant admits to an interview-ending problem, so I always ask. For example, if an interviewee answers this question with, "I get wasted every weekend and come in hung over almost every Monday," you might want to put them in the low-consideration pile. Every now and then, you'll hear an excellent answer, and the applicant gains a few points. Once during an interview, when I asked a young man this question he said, "Well, duh. I'm bald!" A more serious and better answer came when the applicant answered, "I don't speak Spanish, but I'm taking night courses." I practice in San Diego, so this was an excellent response.

4. Get their take on value versus money: "How much money do you think is a lot for dentistry?" If you do a lot of dentistry, you will occasionally have a treatment plan that can be quite expensive. If your applicant thinks $1,000 is a lot of money, you are going to have trouble. It shows in their facial features and body language when the patient asks, "Do I really need this?" Many of the applicants get confused by the question. Try not to give the answer away before they respond, but it's okay to tell them why you asked after they answer.

5. Ask about fees: "Would you feel comfortable discussing fees with a patient?" This is a lead-in question to see if this person will help you sell needed dentistry once you walk out of the room. A follow-up questions might be, "How would you answer the patient if they asked, 'Do I really need this?'"

6. Role-play situations: Ask the applicant, "How would you handle any of the following patient inquiries?"
   A. A patient calls and says, "I'm in pain." What I really want to hear from the applicant is empathy. "I'm so sorry you're in pain.

Tell me about it." Which is a very kind way of finding out the history of the pain to help you schedule better. When a new patient tells their story and hears an empathetic response, they are less likely to call another dentist to see if they can be seen sooner. Having the patient "tell you about it" is an opening to keep the conversation going. The longer the patient stays on the phone (within reason), the more likely they will make their appointment and want to stay with your office. Make sure your applicant has empathy. Often the scheduler's response will be, "Well…we can squeeze you in at 2:30." And I could just see her mouth squeezed like she had eaten a very sour lemon. That grimace can be heard on the phone just as well as a smile can.

B. A patient says, "That is very expensive." So often, the financial person immediately gets defensive explaining material, education, and staffing costs. Once you become defensive, you start to justify your costs. The dentist down the street is cheaper, so why not go there? Should we discuss how we came up with our fees? No, No, No! A better way to handle this is to agree with the patient and get on their side of the table. "Yes, dentistry really is expensive. I wish it were less so." If your applicant gets this wrong, it's an easy fix, but just know you'll need to train them.

C. An insistent sales rep on the phone says, "I need to speak with Dr. Disraeli now." Politeness is the key here. "Thank you so much for calling. Dr. Disraeli usually doesn't handle sales calls during the workday, but he's interested in quite a few things. Can I get a number from you and if he's interested, he'll call back? Or you can email, text, or fax us any information so he can be more informed before he calls." Rudeness to a salesperson tells you a lot about the applicant. And every now and then, the dentist really wants to make the contact. If the bridge has been burned, it's more difficult for the dentist, and word gets out that this office is not nice.

D. A patient asks, "Why am I paying so much when it took so little time?" This is a little tricky and dependent on who is asking. A little humor goes a long way. "I know, Dr. D. is really fast. He's been practicing for a long time to get it just right, and when he does, things go quickly. I'm glad it worked out so well for you." What you don't want to see here is the applicant responding to this question with a thousand-yard stare (looking off in the distance with a frozen appearance). Because then they are obviously wondering themselves why money and time aren't directly linked.

E. A patient asks, "Why don't you take my insurance?" In this era of PPO's, this is a most dangerous question. Your applicant's answer should be something along the lines of, "There are very few dentists who are 'in network' for every plan. Most doctors choose just a few plans that they can work with and try to balance out their practice this way." Basically, you've said nothing while being diplomatic about it.

F. And finally, what to do if a patient wants to know, "Why can't you do a half cleaning if I'm a half hour late?" Basically, you ask this to see how well your interviewees think on their feet. There really isn't a wrong answer unless they're mean or rude. This question doesn't come up very often, but if your applicant is quick, it helps.

7. Encourage thoughtful responses: "Describe your dream job." This can be the biggest golden nugget in your interview. Try not to interrupt as your prospect tells you everything you need to know. In a difficult hiring environment, where there are few applicants and many job offerings, the right applicant will answer in such a way that assures your decision of whether or not to hire them. "I love a job where, once I'm fully trained, my dentist will let me work on my own. I love the one-on-one with the patients."

8. Keep a sense of humor: I like asking the applicant to "Tell me a joke." There are three ways this can go. Most of the time I hear, "I don't know any." I still try to encourage them to think of one. If they still can't come up with something funny, it's neutral and doesn't add or subtract to the interview. If they tell a joke poorly or one that's in bad taste (this is an interview after all), the score of the interview goes down a little. However, if they tell a joke smoothly, the score goes up. Once again, you are trying to see how well someone thinks on their feet and how easy they are to speak with. I once had an incredible applicant tell a racist joke with swear words in the punchline. I was stunned and couldn't respond for a moment. I really wanted to hire her up until then. I think I had the thousand-yard stare.

9. Find their level of commitment: "Have you ever gone above the call of duty? Please explain." What do they consider above the call of duty? Would they do that for you? If they mention that as a hygienist they saw an extra person in the workday...uh oh. This person is trying to pass off a minor change in the schedule as a big deal, worthy of mentioning in an interview. That's like saying "Oh, once, I picked up a piece of paper that someone else had thrown on the floor. I put it in the trash can." On the other hand, if they say that Mrs. Eldergray's ride didn't show up at the end of the day and they volunteered to drive her home because it was on the way, then that's a win. I don't expect my employees to drive patients' home, but if they do, that's way above the pay grade. This is a nice person.

10. Ask about office relationships: "Describe how you would handle a conflict with a fellow employee." What do they consider a conflict? This is really what you're asking. You don't need any unnecessary drama from any one person. If they mentioned a time when "Susie parked in my spot and I had to talk to her after work," you have someone that defines a conflict very lightly. This may not be the right person for you.

11. Ask about patient relationships: "Give a specific example of when you had to deal with a difficult patient." We all know about the patients with gargantuan tongues, or small vertical openings who act like baby birds pointing to their mouths when there is a drop of saliva, or those with lips that move into a tight "O" whenever we get too close. Those patients are tough. I'd really like to know how the interviewee handles the patient who is mean or who asks the same question multiple times waiting for the answer they want. In other words, it's the patient who everyone in the office wants someone else to deal with. For this interview question, pay attention to the body language. Do they shrink backwards in shell shock, or do they lean in, eager to rise to the challenge?

12. Find out how they handle problem solving: "If I wanted to tell your coworkers what they should know about you in order to work well with you, what would I tell them?" This is a bit of a softball question during which your interviewee gets to tell you a little more about themselves. Hopefully it will be something a little different. You might want to emphasize "What will I tell them?" to let them know that you intend to formally introduce them to your staff.

13. Ask about big dreams: "You win $10M in the lottery, what would you do?" If they say they would still work for you, make sure you laugh. The money discussion will tell you something about this person, and it will keep them talking, which is one of the goals of the interview. What person hasn't planned how they'll spend their millions from the lottery? Do they want to buy a house for mom and dad? That means they still have both parents, and they all get along. "I'm going to take a long vacation." Was there mention of a friend or spouse? Is this person a loner? These are subtleties that give you insight into your interviewee's personality, without directly inquiring.

14. Ask about long term goals. "What will you do when you retire?" Most of the people you interview for back-office work are probably many years away from sitting by the fire with a good book, so they don't really know. This might be the first time they've even thought about it. Will it spark more conversation? For those that are a little closer to retirement, you may hear something that will help you connect to this person.

15. Inquire about their job history: "What did you like most about your last job?" Was it the alone time with the patients? I always like when they say that, because I feel the more staff our patients connect with, the more it enhances our practice. Was it the "team feel" in which everyone helps each other out? Wow, someone who likes being a team player. Was it the happy hour every Friday night? Hmm.. perhaps not the thing I was looking for. If they survive the interview and get a job offer, you can tailor your offer to what pleases them, based on answers you receive to this question. And on the flipside, you can ask, "What did you like least? Please complain, I really want to hear it." Unfortunately, most savvy interviewees know this is a trap. Some get clever and try to turn their negatives into a positive with something like, "One of the staff members never cleaned the sterilization room or stocked the rooms during down time. It pulled the rest of the team together and we became a more efficient group because of it.

16. Let them show personal pride: "How will the job you just left be affected by your absence?" I tell them, "Brag a little, let's hear what you do well." This is where you give them a chance to shine in the interview.

17. Ask them to take on integrity: "What does integrity mean to you?" And then ask them to give an example. I run an ethical office and I really want to know if the person I'm interviewing understands the

word. My definition of integrity is doing the right thing when no one is watching.

18. Find out how they feel about punctuality: "How do you rate yourself on time performance?" It's amazing how many people are really honest with this question. The bigger question is what can you (the dentist) tolerate? If you are an "on time" dentist and your applicant says that traffic getting to work makes being on time unpredictable, don't hire this person. Have they never thought to get to work early and grab a coffee, read a book, or call their mother?

19. Encourage reflection: "What part of your work experience have you enjoyed the most?" How does this match up with the answers given so far? We asked about strengths and weaknesses early on, and we keep on asking, just in different ways. It's a red flag if the answers don't match up.

20. Get info on their health records: "Are your immunizations up to date?" This is less an interview question and more learning what you will have to do to get them up to legal speed, as far as immunizations for health care workers are concerned. Make sure that in your state this is a legal question. In some states it's part of the licensure for staff members to be vaccinated for Hepatitis, COVID, etc. If this is your state and this prospect is not vaccinated, why not? And if not, are they willing to get vaccinated?

21. Find out about drugs and addictions: "Would you be willing to take a drug test?" Only ask this if this is legal where you work. If you do ask this, the response should be swift and absolutely positive. If there is any hesitation, ask them why they hesitated. I have never given a drug test, but I always ask just to gauge the speed of the response.

22. Ask about expected compensation: "What compensation are you looking for to start the position?" Sometimes I ask what they would

like to be making in six months or a year from now. How much confidence do they have? I believe it is illegal in most states to ask how much they are making at present or in their last job, but if they volunteer the information, that's up to them. Many of the less experienced candidates will ask what you are offering. Repeat the original question. Do not tell them what you are offering at this time. As a side note, if you are going to hire this person, don't start your relationship off by trying to lowball them. They'll remember that. As a side not, new laws are always being enacted. Please learn the laws In your state before proceeding with an Interview.

23. Ask how high they aim: "What are your objectives regarding this position?" This is a throw away question in that they may not have any objectives for this job at this point, but every now and then, you'll get an honest answer.

24. Ask about handling stress: "What happens if you're under too much pressure?" If they admit to having difficulties and you are a high-level office, don't put yourself in a bad hiring position. Once again check their body language. Are they eager? Or fidgety? Are they unsure how to answer? Maybe holding something back?

25. Find out how they handle work relationships: "How did your last supervisor manage you, and was it effective? Evaluate him or her." This question is if you run a larger office or if they came from a larger office. Look for resentment. Were they happy in a big office? Will they be able to relate to you and your staff if your office is small?

26. Getting to know them: "What interests you outside of work?" We've already asked what isn't on their resume. This is an extension of that original question. Is this person very political and religious or extremely private. How will they fit in with your existing staff? You are building a team, so make sure you hire team players that work well together.

27. Ask about their due diligence: "What do you know about our office?" Did they do any research about you or your staff at all? Did they look at your website? Did they get references from any of your patients or someone in the dental field? Did they read your Yahoo, Yelp, or Google reviews? If they did, it would show up here and their overall score will be higher. This also means the rest of the interview probably went very well.

28. Wrap it up: "What questions do you have?" A lot can be inferred by the questions asked of you. This is always my last question and hopefully the interviewee has lots to ask me.

When you are done, write down some additional notes about this person, giving your overall impressions. I usually take notes during the interview, but I find that when I go over my notes immediately after the interview, I remember more information. If you are doing a lot of interviews, these extra notes will help you keep track of the hierarchy of your applicants. If you're only doing a few, your notes will help you organize your thoughts and assist in training later. Keep in mind, your questions during the interview serve more as a guide than an actual application. Use the questions you feel comfortable with and that give you the best information possible for your practice.

Side note: I am writing this at a time during the COVID 19 pandemic when there is a tremendous labor shortage. In most areas there are fewer job applicants where there used to be many. During times when there are few applicants, only a part of your interview will be true to the original format. The rest of the interview will be a sales job from you to the applicant. You may have only two choices to fill the job, but the applicant has many more dentists looking. Your standards may have to be lowered a bit, and you might have to spend more time training. We all know what the desired end-result should be a trained employee, but we aren't trained in the ways to get there. To help you navigate this, I encourage you to read "The One-Minute Manager" by Ken Blanchard and Spencer Johnson. It is a quick read with very easy instructions, and it offers some swift solutions to some common management issues, especially during these strange pandemic times.

How's the Front Desk Going?

CHAPTER EIGHT

I ended up hiring a woman in her mid-forties. She had two sons in high school, played tennis on the weekends, was married to a contractor, and made baked goods regularly. During her interview, her strength was that she was attending the city college at night. I don't remember her weaknesses. Lola was a very kind, pleasant woman (with great grammar skills...yippee) who got along with everyone. She dressed nicely but perhaps a little too casually (I later learned that the best attire for an office manager was the same thing a bank supervisor might wear). I sat back and let Lola do her thing. My staff seemed to be happy and even Gary thought I had done a good job in hiring Lola.

Lola may have been a touch too nice. Everyone liked her very much. I frequently got compliments about her and requests for her baking recipes. But, she didn't have that drive needed to propel a dental office into the next level.

"Dr. Disraeli's office. This is Lola. How may I help you?"

"This is Alvin Alwayslate. I have an appointment in an hour, and I forgot to put it in my calendar, so I won't be coming in today."

"Okay, Alvin. Is there anything else I can help you with?"

Lola didn't want to embarrass Alvin by reminding him of our late cancellation policy. When she looked up his name during the conversation, the computer flagged his account for several hundred dollars, ninety days overdue. Further information revealed that Alvin canceled frequently at the last minute. Rather than rescheduling Alvin, collecting overdue money, and warning him of our short notice cancellation fees, Lola did what came naturally. She was polite, friendly and used good grammar. Regular baked goods were worth something but not that much. Lola had many good qualities and I thought we could work things out. Training would be important and ongoing.

The question was where should I begin my training of the front office manager? I asked Gary, who laughingly said, "At the beginning." Then he explained that phone calls were the core of the business, the first contact, and home base for questions about money, insurance, scheduling, complaints, and lots more. Although the new patient phone call was probably the most important, it also paved the way for more in-person interactions. We started with the phone call.

You may have the most empathetic and kind person answering the phone, but there are still some nuances that are necessary to give a new patient the gentle nudge needed to make an appointment. A new patient really doesn't want to hear a sales pitch, but there are certain phrases that work well after a connection has been made. The connection is established with active listening, which is a way of listening that assures the other person that you *are* listening. The other person doesn't want to get the impression that you are tuning out the words while you watch the dust motes dancing in the light. They want to feel like you are looking them in the eye through the phone.

There are a few tips that will help you become an active listener, with the first and foremost being that you actually have to listen to what the other person is saying. The primary tip is to repeat what the person said to you. If it's a long explanation or conversation, repeat just the last sentence or two. It will work better, though, if you summarize using your own words.

"Good morning, Dr. Disraeli's office. This is Lola. How may I help you?"

"Hi Lola. This is Greg Nomad and I just moved to town and I'm looking for a new dentist."

"Hi Greg. Welcome to our city! Where was your last home?" At this point, Lola has acknowledged that Greg is new to town, and she has shown that she is a positive person. Her question about his last home serves two purposes. First, it gets him to keep talking, which will give Lola a chance to figure out how to guide him into joining our practice. Second, it gets him talking about himself, which is his favorite subject. Lola will need to know certain information that will be easier to get once a rapport has been established. The patient will understand that even though we are a business, we are human as well.

"I just moved here from Seattle." Okay, so Greg isn't a big talker.

"Wow, Seattle is pretty far away from here." Repeating the name of the city is active listening. Lola could have just asked her next question, but having Greg know that she is unrushed and interested is more important.

"Did you have a dentist who took care of you there?" With his short answer it sounds like we should get down to business. We need to figure out if there were x-rays, and if so, which ones and when. We need to know if he has insurance. It would be nice to know if it was the same insurance that he had in Seattle, since it would be easier to take a full set of x-rays if the insurance was different and there weren't timing restrictions. Before setting him up for a prophylaxis, it would be nice to know when his teeth were last cleaned and how often he feels they need cleaning. There are a lot of other personal things that would be nice to know, which we could use in the future to help him feel more integrated with the office. But there is plenty of time for the rest of that.

"Yeah, I had a dentist that I saw a couple times a year." Well, that answers a few of the questions.

"It sounds like you have been taking care of your teeth." Active and positive listening. "Do you just need an exam or are you also due for a cleaning?" This lets him know, gently, that an exam is the priority. It's amazing how many people just want a cleaning.

"Well, the last time I got them cleaned, the hygienist said I needed a deep cleaning, which I'm a little confused about since I'm really good with brushing and I go in twice a year." Hallelujah. He just gave us more to work with. Now is not the time to get into a discussion about deep cleaning or the inference that he wasn't fully convinced he needed it. A note should be taken to inform the hygienist and dentist about his concerns. That way when the patient shows up for the first visit, even if he forgot about this conversation, we can show that we communicate efficiently.

"It sounds like you're very diligent, but dentistry can be a little confusing sometimes." Active listening. "Dr. Disraeli is very good at explaining things in an easy way. I think you're really going to like it here." This is the gentle nudge needed to get the new patient moving towards making an appointment. "Would you like an appointment for an exam and get started on your cleaning needs?"

"Sure." Still not very talkative.

"Before we get to a time and date that will work for you, may I ask a few more important questions?" Once the appointment has been made, the patients don't feel a real need to continue with data gathering, so let's save the dessert for the end.

"Okay."

"Do you have insurance that we can help bill for you?" If the answer is no, then you need to give him a realistic accounting of the fees involved for the first visit, even though you don't know what it will be, yet. If he has a PPO or an insurance that you are unfamiliar with, it would be very efficient to get as much information about the insurance before he comes in the first time Then you can only give him an estimate of the fees he is expected to pay. If he has a DMO (dental based HMO) and it's one you don't accept (and I hope you don't), then he needs to know now.

"Yes, I've just started a new job. I'm not sure of the name, but the HR department told me it was a good one and I don't have to go to a specific dentist." So not a DMO, but this might be all the information we'll get until he comes in. One piece of good news is that we don't have to work with previous charges against his maximums or restrictions on treatment like x-rays. There are a few software programs (like Trojan) that will tell you the probable insurance if you know the employer, and then you can get more information like dates of last cleaning, exam and x-rays as well as what type of x-rays. In this case, it's a new insurance and you can start from scratch.

"In that case, just get us the insurance information as soon as you can so we can help you the best way we can. Will that be alright?" Always asking questions.

"Yeah, I guess." Wow. Enthusiastic and wordy.

"Great. Would you like to know a little about how most insurances work?"

"Yeah, I guess."

"When you come in for a full exam with x-rays and a cleaning, the cost will be $322.00. But with insurance, this visit is _usually_ covered at one hundred percent. Without knowing which insurance you have, I can't tell you if there is a copayment, a deductible, or a preset maximum that they will pay, which is why I wanted to let you know the full fee." The full set of x-rays was assumed, and if Greg didn't correct you, this often-contested part of the exam should be accepted without argument. At the same time, Greg is being told that if his insurance doesn't pay, he will be responsible for the full amount. This is an incentive for Greg to get that information to you quickly. Now it's time for the final question.

"Greg what day works best for you?" Please note that Lola didn't ask Greg when he would like to come in. That is a question that is **too** open ended.

Sometimes a new patient needs a little nudge or encouragement to make the appointment. When you go to a restaurant and can't make up your mind between two possibilities, you ask the server for some help. "I can't decide between the Rocky Mountain oysters and the escargot..." mused the diner.

"This might surprise you, but we get so many requests for the oysters that we usually run out. They are a delight worth ordering." encouraged the waiter, as his face lit up. Compare that to this response where he says, "They're both very good," in a deadpan voice while tapping the tablet with his pencil.

"Hmm, I better order the French fries."

In our example above with Greg, at some point the scheduler needs to make a declarative sentence that almost dares the patient to refuse. "Dr. Disraeli is a superb dentist." Of course, the patient knows that the scheduler is being paid to say this, but with a little enthusiasm, along with a smile (which the caller can hear, and if you don't believe me, do an experiment with your staff members), the patient can comfortably go along with the story. A few more encouraging statements include:

"You are going to love it here."

"Dr. D. is a very kind dentist."

"I bring my kids here."

"Dr. D. just exudes trust."

"Dr. D. will not rush you."

Even if the patient suspects the scheduler is being paid to say encouraging words, it's a lot better than saying nothing. Your enthusiasm will burst through the phone.

"Tuesdays work best for me," Greg replied.

"That works out well for us too. Will next Tuesday, the 19th at 10:00 work for you?"

"Unfortunately, not at that time. Do you have anything in the early afternoon?"

"Not on that day, but on the following Tuesday, the 26th, I have a 1:00 appointment available. Will that work for you?"

"Yeah, okay."

"Two more things. I have your email address, so I will send you the forms we need to have filled out by the time you come in" Direct the caller to your website for online registration. "And the last thing is that if we have a change in our schedule (never say cancellation—we don't want to give Greg any ideas that it's okay to cancel) and can get you in next Tuesday, would you like me to call you?"

"That would be great. I'm going on a trip to Europe at the end of the month and I would love to get things going sooner."

Lola wrote this down so she could ask him more about his trip when she saw him next. She also wrote more notes to give to the staff so Greg would feel like his new dental office was aware of his needs and would take care of him.

"Europe is great this time of year." More active listening. "I'm really looking forward to seeing you on the 26th. Good-bye."

After all that, Lola would try as hard as she could to make the afternoon of the 16th work for Greg, which was his first choice for an appointment to begin with.

So, a few points in this conversation to keep in mind:

A. Employ active listening.

B. Keep great personal notes and use the information you've heard during this call.

C. Always ask questions to keep the patient communicating and hopefully build rapport.

D. Make encouraging comments to instill patient confidence in your practice. Things like, "You are going to love it here," or "I bring my family here," or "Dr. D. is very thorough, patient, meticulous…" or whatever the patient needs to hear in the moment. Always be encouraging and nurturing.

E. Instead of answering questions with a single word, ask follow-up questions to get the patient to reveal more about themselves. The more they reveal, the less likely they will try someplace else.

The Incoming Calls

CHAPTER NINE

Have you actually sat down with the person answering phones and given explicit instructions on what you want? Probably not. But doing so will make your life much easier. Write down every possible situation for a phone call and decide how you would like it to be handled. Let's start with another new patient call:

The phone rings, and your scheduler answers, "Dr. Disraeli's office!" Wow! What a statement.

The patient waits a beat, is he supposed to talk or wait for a question...? "Hi, my name is Waldo Winkle. I saw your postcard about a special deal for a first-time patient."

"Yes." Was that an affirmation that his name was Waldo or a question about a special deal?

"Uh, can I come in to see Dr. Disraeli?"

"I have an opening on Thursday at 11:00." Wait! What about the deal? "Okay, I'll be there."

"What's your name please?"

"Waldo Winkle," he says with a sigh.

Obviously, this is an exaggerated example of the scheduler being uninterested in the success of the practice. There has been a total disconnect between the dentist and what the receptionist is supposed to say. It is the dentist's fault for not practicing a script and for perhaps putting the wrong person in a place to make a first impression. The phone call is how the patient decides if they *want* to come in. The receptionist needs to make the patient feel wanted.

"Good morning, Dr. Disraeli's office. How may I help you?"

The greeting is neutral, efficient, and quick. By asking a question, the receptionist is initiating conversation, and she will continue to ask questions until it's time to hang up.

"Hi, my name is Waldo Winkle, I live close to your office, and I saw your postcard about a special deal for first time patients."

"Yes, we sent them out to many of your neighbors as well, Waldo. Our office just opened, and we are trying to let everyone know. Do you have any specific questions, or would you like to take advantage of the special offered on the postcard?"

Waldo's name was used because everyone likes to hear their name, and it proved the receptionist was listening (I suggest trying to use it at least three times in this initial phone call depending on the length of the call). This also elicits enthusiasm, excitement, and a feeling of ownership in the office as if the spouse of the doctor was on the phone.

"I haven't had my teeth looked at in…well…quite a while."

"Then I'm very glad you chose us. Welcome back to dentistry. We will take excellent care of you. Dr. Disraeli is an excellent dentist, and our staff is extremely well trained. I can't wait for you to meet us, Waldo. When were you thinking of coming in?"

The patient admitted poor dentistry and instead of reprimanding him for his poor past decisions, the response was a positive welcome and a promise to treat him well. His name was used again, forming an even stronger connection. Bragging about the doctor and the staff shows confidence, which is very attractive. It is not "the staff" but "our staff," which shows the receptionist is part of the team. The question at the end assumes that Waldo is interested, which again instills confidence, but it would be arrogance if the receptionist hadn't already established rapport.

There are some consultants who believe that a longer phone conversation equates to a better first visit. Questions asked by the receptionist indicate active listening with no apparent rush. When there are two or more people answering the phones, this is easy and wonderful. However, in a smaller office, you need the skill to shorten the call after an appropriate duration. Patients will recognize the need to be efficient and will appreciate that you are busy, but not too busy to use their name and give them something to look forward to.

I mentioned active listening in the last paragraph and the previous chapter. I want to expand on that because it is something the entire staff and dentist need to do as a matter of habit. Active listening is when you respond to a statement or question by repeating (in your own words) a portion of what you heard the person say before you answer or respond. It proves that the person was heard and they will pay attention to the response more attentively. For example…

"Doctor D. that crown you just placed hurts when I eat," the patient shares.

You nod empathetically. "The tooth hurts when you chew. Is it sensitive to temperature as well?"

Or…

A patient calls and says, "I can't come in today, I'm sick."

"I'm so sorry you're not feeling well," the scheduler responds. "Do you feel up to rescheduling now or should I call you next week?"

At this point, the patient knows that you listened and is eager to answer your question. It will be a lot easier to figure out the issue if you both work on it, and you'll both enjoy the process more. If you don't make a connection, you pave the way for trouble. I have actually heard the following conversation between patient and dentist:

Patient: "My tongue is still numb, and you took out that wisdom tooth over a week ago."

Dentist: "Well, you signed the informed consent."

Do you think the patient went to her attorney or did a yelp review first?

Okay, now that we have learned how to be an active listener, let's put it to use by looking at a small sample of the possible incoming calls:

1. **The new patient procedure:** When a new patient calls, collect as much data as you can on the phone, and then keep a cheat sheet on

the patient to prepare yourself for the first face-to-face meeting. You already know to be enthusiastic, ask questions, and use the patient's name to give the impression of ownership. But the patient will often slip something personal into the call like an upcoming vacation, so a later appointment would be appreciated. Or wanting an appointment on Wednesday, so her husband can watch their kids. When you write this personal information down, you can ask questions about the vacation or the ages of the kids when the patient arrives for the first visit. You will look really good *and* bring the new patient closer to finding your office indispensable—and when you make a mistake (aren't we all human?), the patient will tolerate it much more, *because they like you.*

2. **An insurance question:** When a patient asks, "Do you take my insurance?" The short answer is, "Yes, we bill all insurances unless you have an HMO. Do you have a dental HMO, also called a DMO?" Wait for a response. If they have an HMO, be polite, informative, and apologetic. If they have a PPO that we don't accept, ask, "Do you know how your insurance works?" If the answer is no, you say, "Let me explain the difference between in-network and out-of-network. The in-network DDS signs a contract to accept a lower fee dictated by the insurance, and in return, the insurance company recommends the DDS. We are not on that list, but we can take care of billing your insurance for you as a service that we provide. We understand that not every dentist takes every PPO, so we offer a same-day discount to help offset the difference. Both you and the insurance get a break." At this point, assume they want to make an appointment. "You are going to love it here. If not, you can take the dentist out back and hit him or her. Use a book so it leaves no marks." (Adding humor makes it feel like the scheduler is on the patient's side.) "Let me have all your insurance info so I can get set before you come in. Do you need a cleaning or just an exam?" (Once again, note that the exam was assumed as an absolute.) "Afternoon

or morning? Is Wednesday good for you?" If the conversation goes back to in-network, let them know there are some good dentists on the plan as well as some that might not be. "The important thing is that you see a dentist and if you would like help picking from a list, let me know. I won't tell you who the bad ones are, and unfortunately bad reputations travel faster than good ones, but if we recognize someone who is reputable, we can let you know. Dr. Disraeli is not constrained by insurance limitations and will only do the best for you. He treats and diagnoses as if you were his family." At this point, you need to make sure the patient knows his copayment is estimated. Share that you're estimating high, but you will get the proper amount by the time they arrive (that's if you have all the correct insurance info plus a day or two before the appointment). Get the patient in ASAP, and get all the insurance maximums, deductibles, and schedules of payment. And don't forget to use your cheat sheet for personalization.

In my office, I offer a ten percent discount for out- of-network patients who pay their portion on the day of the appointment. We then explain that this is often the difference between the costs of the PPO and a non-PPO, and it helps a little.

3. **The patient who winces at price:** Sometimes a patient pins you down far enough to insist on a quote on the spot, and then replies, "Wow that is expensive." In response, don't get angry or defensive, just simply say, "Yes, dentistry is expensive." And then shut up. Once you start trying to explain your fees, you start to backpedal, and it sounds like an excuse. It's better to be empathetic and agree when a patient says it costs a lot.

4. **Quoting prices over the phone:** If a patient asks (for example), "How much is a crown?" over the phone, don't tell them. Instead ask questions like:

   "Have you been diagnosed by a dentist?"

"Do you know which tooth needs the crown?"

"When was the last time you were seen?"

We try very hard not to give prices over the phone because we don't want to get in the '*shopping*' game. We also haven't had a chance to create value with the patient. Sometimes patients ask the price before they come in because they feel they are supposed to. But instead, we give them reassurance that they have made the right choice regardless of price. "Dr. Disraeli is excellent with crowns!" The only price I *want* them to know is the cost of the first visit or the amount their insurance won't pay on that visit. If a new patient is demanding and really wants to know the cost of a crown, and you have deflected as much as possible, give them the range. But make sure they know there is no diagnosis, and you don't want to be held to that fee. A less expensive treatment might be done, the risks of a crown might be too high, or other things might be needed in addition to a crown. I would often offer a courtesy exam (not including x-rays) to get them in the door, and then I would make sure we do everything possible so they stay as a patient. Getting them in the door should be your goal, but sometimes a demanding patient really isn't worth the disruption to the office.

5. **The patient who insists on just cleaning as a first-time patient:** If a patient says, "I only want a cleaning," agree that this is desirable and why (money, time, inconvenience of hearing bad news), but also give the counterpoint. "But Dr. Disraeli likes to practice dentistry, and he does it ethically. It is against the law to have a hygienist see a patient without an exam and a recommendation by a dentist. Have you had x-rays recently that will help us?" Then keep the information coming with questions like, "Are you new to San Diego?" "Yes? Well, where are you from?"

6. **The fearful patient:** If a patient admits he or she is scared, acknowledge the courage it took to make the call to see a dentist in the first

place. Ask if there is anything specific that they fear and acknowledge that as well. After hearing all their fears, decide how to proceed. If you go too fast, you might lose them, so I offer a courtesy exam where nothing will cause pain. If they feel up to it, include x-rays for the normal charge. Mention the various methods we have, including, verbal anesthesia–"Dr. Disraeli will listen to you." Some offices don't want to do this and don't want these patients. Make sure your office manager knows your limits. Make SURE you repeat that the new patient "will love it here," to all of your staff, so that they will repeat it to your patients.

7. **The patient in pain:** The patient says, "This toothache/lost temporary/occlusal adjustment, [etc.] really hurts!"

   These things can be very painful. If that's the case, the first thing they want to hear is acknowledgement of the discomfort. If it's a new toothache, be empathetic; "I'm so sorry you're in pain. Tell me about it." Then be an active listener. Take notes so the patient doesn't have to tell the story again to the assistant and then the dentist. If it is severe, get them in ASAP and as early in the day as possible so that a referral can be given if necessary. If you know it must be referred, don't waste your time, and refer them out immediately. Never say we will squeeze you in, as that makes someone feel like they won't get one hundred percent of the dentist's attention. Regardless, it's okay to let the patient know that you and your staff are busy at that time. "Our office is currently busy, and you may need to wait just a little, but Dr. Disraeli will focus on you when he sees you." Once again, have the conversation between the dentist and the scheduler to enforce your preferences.

8. **The angry patient:** At some point, you will have to deal with an angry patient, whether it's your fault or not. No matter what happens, you must be an active listener. Learn to repeat the last sentence you hear the patient say, but in a slightly different way and with a

question. "So, the hygienist poked you too hard?" Make sure the patient knows you are taking him seriously (and not being sarcastic), and wait until they are done speaking before asking, "How can I make it right?" The type of office you run determines your remedy–Nordstrom vs. Walmart. Strive to be Nordstrom. In our office, we listen to a patient's grievance, acknowledge their concern, and then solve the problem beyond the patients' expectations. Afterward, when they call to tell us they're happy with the outcome, it's one of the best phone calls we can receive, because we're proud of how we handled a tricky situation.

In the case of a hygiene failure, after listening to the patient and acknowledging them, we offer a courtesy cleaning, either for that visit or the next (or refund insurance money). Absolutely do not make this sound routine or like something we do for anyone who asks. This goes a long way and tells the patient that we take them seriously. Of course, some patients are complainers and after multiple attempts to appease them, they are never happy. Should we let them fall through the cracks? ("Oops, I forgot to make your next appointment.") This is a decision that the dentist needs to make, and it should not be taken lightly. Most importantly, we take every complaint seriously.

9. **The pre-medication or pregnant patient:** Pre-medication rules have changed a lot in the last few years. It used to be an absolute that we gave antibiotics an hour before any visit where the patient had a mitral valve prolapse, artificial or partly artificial joints, recent surgery, artificial heart valve, pins and plates, or any time an MD thought it was important. We handled this by insisting that every patient get the premed until they brought in an exception note from their MD. We were covered legally at that point, but we were over-prescribing antibiotics. Luckily, the pre-medication rules have softened, so there are far fewer reasons to medicate patients. However,

there are still a few absolutes that need premed until their physician takes responsibility and writes, emails, or texts a note saying there is no further need. Since the need for antibiotic pre-medication is not only a legal need but a medical one, do not allow yourself to be bullied by a patient who insists it isn't necessary. Patients cannot legally sign something that absolves the dentist of responsibility.

For almost all pregnant patients we have permission from their OBs to do anything necessary. However, that doesn't mean you should. As dentists we are fairly certain we use nothing that will cause birth defects or spontaneous miscarriages, and we are legally protected by the permission the OB gives (in writing) to treat their patient. But the only thing we do that is above reproach is a routine prophylaxis, and even then we ask permission for fluoride paste to polish the teeth. When something restorative is needed, try to evaluate the possibility of waiting a year. If you think harm will come by stalling, then treat the tooth or teeth, but even then, try to stall until late in the second or third trimester. If there is a birth defect or anything even remotely serious and you did dental work, the mother is going to blame herself for thinking she was more important than her future baby, and then she will blame you no matter how ludicrous the validity of the claim. She might feel that the stress of the dental work was harmful and caused the issue. The conversation should be, "Mrs. Glowing, your OB will probably tell you that dentistry is okay, but we like to be very conservative at this time. We try to evaluate if the tooth will decline to the point of causing an infection, which has a higher potential of causing distress to your baby, or if we think we can wait until after you deliver and get a chance to bond with your baby. In this case, the potential for increased damage if we wait is high, so I am recommending..." On the other hand, pregnancy gingivitis is very common, and we often recommend more cleanings during this time. The explanation is that plaque is an infection, and your body uses inflammation to battle the infection. Removing the plaque more frequently (one extra time) will make things not only more comfortable, but healthier as well.

10. **Short cancellation:** You need to gauge the patient as to why the cancellation occurred. If this is a frequent event, discuss the cancellation fee. A cancellation fee is something that was agreed upon when the patient first signed an informed consent to be treated in your office. It is an absolute statement that says, "You will be charged $100 (or whatever your office choses) for every hour that you miss without twenty-four hours prior notice," This is also the area that says we charge 1.5% interest on all accounts over ninety days (check your local laws for legal restrictions and language). In reality, we are never absolute, even though it sounds like we are. When a patient has a stupid reason for cancelling at the last minute or not showing up, we remind them of the cancellation fee and then say this one instance was your freebie, but we can't continue to be forgiving in the future, and then we follow up on that. You can always rescind the fee later, but it is better to be a little more forceful up front and be lenient later than to waste a lot of time. Even Nordstrom charges late fees and interest. For non-stupid reasons regarding last minute cancelling, be kind. Things like traffic, a sick child, or being ridiculously busy at work are easier excuses to be nice. Your alternative is to basically call the patient a liar or to let them know that this office has no heart. Do you need to charge them? Do you need to warn them that this one was a courtesy cancellation with no charge? Or is it a legitimate reason that we need to be sympathetic to? We might as well take an inevitable situation and use it for PR. Be careful that the person answering phones doesn't feel the need to teach a lesson.

11. **The sick patient:** Your first and foremost duty is to your staff. If the patient is sick and even slightly contagious, re-schedule. If this is a frequent event, discuss the cancellation fee.

12. **Confirming appointments:** (Yes, there are still patients that want confirmation via phone). All hygiene patients are booked in advance and when the appointment is booked we encourage the patient to immediately put the date into their phone or planner if possible. You need to establish a comfort zone with communication. What does the patient prefer: phone calls, texts, email, pony express, or postcards? Once you establish a formula for reminders, you need to keep it consistent. You don't want your patient saying, "Yeah, I uh didn't come in because you forgot to call and remind me yesterday." Communicate a week before the appointment via the patient's pre-ferred method with something like, "We're looking forward to seeing you next Tuesday, July 14, at 9:00 a.m. If there are any problems with this appointment, please let us know." Another communication a day before (or if the appointment is on Monday, the last day of the pre-vious week) should be plenty of notice. Some patients will complain that this is too much or too little. Adapt to your individual patients.

13. **Failed appointments:** A failed appointment is when a scheduled patient is a no-show without any notice. If that happens, here is a tried-and-true procedure you can use.

    A. Make a call to the patient seven to fifteen minutes after they're a no show and ask, "Are you okay?"

    B. If they don't answer, leave a message saying, "You have missed your appointment today. We are concerned. Please contact us to let us know you are okay."

    C. Note in the chart all that applies and include the time of the appointment. Do not forget this step. Once a patient starts arguing with you a year later, it's easy to say, "Let me look in your chart."

    D. Determine whether or not to charge a fee.

E. Flag it as a failure in the schedule/computer so it will automatically go to the quick call list (QCL).

F. Go through the QCL every month starting with the newest first. Call, email, text, post card. Keep notes on the QCL and keep it rolling.

G. Send a letter after two months that includes, "Hey, we missed you. Let us know what is going on or if your problem has been taken care of. One way or another, please get in touch with us so we can figure out what to do."

H. Send another letter at month four similar to the previous one. If they still ghost you after all that, then let it go.

14. **The patient who wants to change appointments:** This should always be done with a smile in your voice. "It is our pleasure to be a full-service office." Consider the alternative; being curt with someone who is trying to change an existing appointment. There is no gain to being mean or overly instructive, it's going to happen anyway so once again, turn it into a PR windfall. There will occasionally be a patient who annoys the hell out of you because of frequent changes. This is the patient who knows they bug you, but the kinder you are, the more likely they will refer their friends to see you. Some patients will say they need to change appointments but won't do it right then. Never let a patient go without something on the books, even if it is a tickler. "Mr. Better-Late, if I don't hear from you in one week, I'll give you a call." Keep in mind that people remember how you make them feel more than anything.

15. **Scheduling regular appointments:** You need to remember that this is where your business comes from, and a smile should be in the voice of the scheduler. We really are looking forward to seeing them because this is what we do. Without them, we wouldn't be here. They are not annoying us by calling when we would rather be solving a

crossword puzzle or filing our nails. This is when we perk up and show off our professionalism with a touch of kindness.

Phone skills are merely one piece of a larger puzzle but a very important one. If your receptionist is more clueless than empathetic, you will need to correct this. The careless, carefree receptionist is not trainable. I believe that with positive reinforcement you can change people a little, but uncaring people present too large of a leap. Make a change if you are constantly listening so that you can gauge kindness and empathy. There's a reason you're listening so carefully. Kindness and empathy should always be there, and you should be able to trust your receptionist without constant vigilance.

There are a lot of seminars available for front office verbal training (bring your back-office staff too). The important thing to realize is that there is training available for interpersonal skills. You may have a receptionist who can make the computer dance, and as a result, all of the day sheets are perfect. But it's the connections your staff makes to people that will fill the schedule. Make changes in your personnel to match each staff member's most important skills with the right job.

At an upcoming office meeting, write out several of the above sample phone scenarios and ask your staff to name some more. After they've done this, go over a few ways you want them answered and then get staff input for the rest.

You can't have a staff that is too well trained. Customer service and patient empathy should always be a work-in-progress for your dental practice.

Stones in My Pocket

CHAPTER TEN

I was ten years out of school, three years on my own, and feeling good about my practice. In fact, I was feeling more confident about my dentistry and my team. What I wasn't confident about was the amount of work I had left to do. It was the feeling that I had done all the dentistry on all of my patients and the next month would be dry. What would I do then? I was lucky because the next month went just fine. But what about the following month? I had scoured all my patients and diagnosed everything possible. Oh sure, I still diagnosed the occasional cavity, broken tooth, or failed restoration from a hygiene exam, but that felt like I was mopping up crumbs. I was averaging eight to ten new patients a month. There was always some diagnosis from that, but the feeling of impending doom never went away.

I called my best friend and classmate from dental school who practiced in Beverly Hills. I told Andy of my angst and he laughed at me. He said I was going to be in the top five percent of dentists because of my worries. That made no sense to me, and I got a little frustrated at his response.

"Explain," I demanded.

"Sure," he replied. "Happy to help. "You worry because you care. In fact, you care enough to call someone and ask for help. Luckily, you called me. I happen to be smarter than you because I went through this six months ago. I called *you* then, but you were busy bonding with your third son who had just been born, and you said you'd call me back. You understandably forgot. So, I called my uncle, a retired dentist. He wanted to do lunch. We went to that new Thai restaurant on Rodeo."

"Really?" I asked with a tinge of sarcasm. "Ya wanna tell me what you ate, too?"

"Sorry," he apologized, realizing he was getting off-track. "Anyway, it turns out that a lot of potentially successful dentists go through the same thing as what you're going through now. But here's the secret sauce: The worry that *not everything will work out* is the spur that kicks you into a higher gear. All you have to do is face that worry and refuse to let it take over."

"How?" I asked, still a bit confused.

"You ask questions, you experiment, and you keep it at the top of your mental to-do list. Basically, your fear of failure helps you think of ideas to improve your practice. It makes you seek out help from outside sources to become more efficient, get more new patients, and hold on to your existing patients. Some dentists are content to stay where they are, and they don't grow. They are too afraid to make changes because they barely make enough money to pay their bills. Making changes is too risky, so they don't do it."

"So, my paranoia will make me a better dentist?" I wondered aloud.

"When dentists look ahead, many see themselves getting more successful year after year. They think that what they have done in the past is a recipe that will insure a better, happier practice in the future. Most have done fairly well in spite of themselves. They're satisfied about their past accomplishments, but they don't pay attention to the rocky details that got them there."

"And my paranoia?"

"Allows you to keep checking the past and learning from it. It shows you are not resting on your rear molars waiting for things to happen."

"Okay, I get it. My paranoia is my superpower."

"Yup."

We talked for a little longer and he gave me some more advice that I thought was silly, but hey, best friend and all, right? I heard him out. He admitted he was skeptical about this advice at first, but his uncle said it had worked for him for years.

"Uncle Svengali told me there are two main things we, as dentists, forget to do on a regular basis. The first is getting new patients. In the beginning, you *subtly* make sure every person you meet knows you're a dentist who welcomes new patients."

"Yeah, I know," I agreed. "When I meet someone new, I always ask what they do, which leads them to ask what I do. I tell them I'm a dentist and then I get enthusiastic about it. I tell them I get to meet new people all the time and get to satisfy my compulsive need to be the best I can."

"Exactly. Coincidentally, I do the same thing," he replied. "However, I don't always remember to do it. It's not a habit because I don't meet new (non-patient) people every day," he admitted. "The other way to get new patients is by asking your existing patients to send their friends and family your way."

"I learned a new technique for that," I interrupted. "At the end of their appointment, I thank them for coming in to see me and then give them a compliment. Most people will compliment you back. When they do, I say something like, 'I'm so glad you said that because I'm always looking for new patients, and happy patients are my best referral source. If you know of anyone who needs a dentist, please think of me.' Sometimes you just know that conversation isn't right, so I ask for an online review instead. They almost always say sure they'll write one, but even though their intentions are good, their execution drops over time. They usually forget by the time they close the office door. Whenever I get a commitment for a review, I immediately go to my office and send them a letter thanking them in advance for their review," I said proudly, thinking I was doing an incredible job of internal marketing.

"That's a great idea," my friend said. "I am definitely going to do that. But let me ask you a question."

"Sure," I said smugly. I was happy to give him advice for a change. "Do you ever forget to do this? To compliment your patients and then ask for referrals?"

I had forgotten that forgetting was the topic. "Yes," I said sadly.

"Indeed!" he said like a know-it-all. "Me too." I felt less like an idiot. "Before we talk about how to fix this, I want to tell you the second thing we forget to do. It's getting more diagnoses."

"But I always look for more diagnoses. It's pretty much my entire life," I countered.

"Sure, but there are circumstances in which you don't go the extra step needed. For example, let's say you're running late on a prophy check, and you see something. It's not major but you're unsure if it's something new. Chances are that you don't make your hygienist run late and you don't want to run late for that patient who has already been topicaled and waiting for anesthesia. In the back of your mind you tell yourself, "I'll remember this and talk to her about it on her next visit."

"Yeah. I know I've done that," I confessed. "I usually forget about it until the next visit, and the same thing happens again."

"Same here. Another example is that a patient who exhausts you with questions and wants proof that is difficult—not impossible, but difficult—to provide. Let's say a previous dentist had placed a crown and the margins are not great. You've been waiting for more evidence even though stalling could allow decay to run to the nerve. Is it worth the few hundred net dollars you'll get to convince this skeptic that a new crown is in his best interests?"

"Well, when you put it like that, no. But aren't we supposed to be able to sleep at night knowing we've done the right thing?" I asked.

"Absolutely. So why do we let these things slide? It's not because we don't care, it's because we forget. Sometimes it's on purpose because we let things gently slide out of focus and move on. Sometimes we're a touch lazy or we're feeling insecure one day. We're so busy that day that we forget tomorrow is only lightly scheduled."

"And your solution?" I asked.

"Uncle Svengali said to put a heavy stone in your pocket. He used the stone, because it was slightly uncomfortable and kept the task in his immediate attention. Attach a task to the weight of the stone. If you need more new patients, the weight of the stone will focus you towards getting new patients. Then you'll recognize opportunities to ask existing patients for new patients quicker, and therefore you'll do so. Instead of saying to yourself after the patient left, 'Wow, I should've asked her for a referral. She was mentioning a cousin moving into town.' With the heavy stone in your pocket, you would have been primed and ready to let her know you would be thrilled if her cousin came to you as a dentist. If you need more diagnoses, the stone represents looking for more work. When that crack on the amalgam filling comes along, you'll be prepared to either spend the necessary time or reschedule that patient for more time on the next visit. And when it comes to that *difficult-to-convince* patient, you'll take a deep breath and plow on."

"I'm assuming the heavy stone is a metaphor," I asked hopefully.

"Well, yes and no. It really could be a stone, or a large piece of paper or even a sticker on your watch," he clarified. "It just needs to be a big reminder, but Uncle Svengali said you need to limit the time you use it, or the 'power' will wear off. You'll stop noticing that it's there because you'll get used to it."

"Okay? Then when do we use it?" I asked.

"Whenever you notice the schedule is light or you have fewer new patients than you want, go for the stone."

"So, it's only for those two scenarios?" I asked, even though I knew the answer.

"Not necessarily. Let me show you another example," he offered. "You know how hard it is to change an officewide procedure after being introduced to it at a seminar, right? The new concept seems so exciting to you, and you think that on Monday when you present it to your staff they'll also love it and it'll be a done deal—only to realize that by the following Monday things go back to where they originally were. The stone can help remind you to give positive feedback when you make a big change, encouraging everyone when they utilize the *new system*. When you do a review of an employee and you want to change their behavior *just a little*, remembering to give positive feedback is important. I'm sure a smart guy like you can think of a few more examples for the stone."

"I hope so. Thank you very much," I offered sincerely. "I've just realized I'm in the top percentage of dentists because I'm forgetful and insecure. Now I have some solutions to problems I didn't know I had. Plus, I have a really good friend!"

This lesson is very important for those of us that are, for example, creating new content for our website while worrying about an employee who is not working out. We are performing an excellent exam, and at the same time we are searching for ways to give legitimate positive reinforcement to bolster the rest of the staff. Basically, we are busy, and we need to figure out a way to motivate ourselves to keep our practices growing. The "stones in my pocket" philosophy is one way to use your worry and fear to remind you what you need to do (specific to your practice) in order to grow and move forward.

Everyone Has a Saying

CHAPTER ELEVEN

The office shifted personalities as my employees found their way. I got a little more confident in my managerial skills. Some employees moved on while new ones moved in. Eventually, I figured it was time to have a mission statement. This was the 1990's and everyone was creating one. The consultants insisted that if you didn't have something spelled out for your staff, your office would flail about like a halibut in a shallow puddle. I read over some of the samples and felt they weren't complete enough. There was a suggestion that to create a mission statement you should have an office meeting with everyone participating, get their ideas, fine tune the language, and come up with your masterpiece.

So that's what I did, and it was a great office meeting. I catered it and went a little overboard with the celebration, but everyone had a good time. We had an easel with a large flipchart, so the office manager (who had the best handwriting) wrote down all the suggestions with a big smile and enthusiasm. We debated over major concepts and individual words, then we argued over which sentence was more important, and because of its value, if it should be at the beginning or end of the statement. We even dealt with the font, the framing, and the size of the entire display. It was a great team building exercise. We just knew that our patients would be impressed with our professionalism and as a result, flood us with new patients. We hung it in the hall exactly where we planned and where both patients and staff could see it.

I'm certain that I read it at least once after it was hung. I'm not certain that anyone else ever did.

I knew there was probably a better way to use the mission statement, but after I read it on the wall, I felt a little embarrassed by it. It seemed cheesy, overly sentimental, hokey, and syrupy. What did my patients think when they read this? Did they gloss over it, thinking, "Oh, really? Not another mission statement. I don't think I can force my eyes to read the whole thing." Did they see our superlatives (excellence, best quality, incredible staff) and have a few of their own? Such as, "That is *incredibly* trite," or "That statement is the world's *worst* idea." After a year or two, I took down the mission statement, put it in my closet, and promptly forgot about it. No one noticed.

A while later I realized that I kept repeating the same expressions. I had been saying them for a few years, but I started repeating them more frequently. It felt a little like the mission statement, but it was never posted, and it didn't feel "created" or forced. One of the staff members once wrote down my repeated sayings, along with a betting pool as to how many times would I repeat the same phrase and which one I would say the most. I found out about it after a few months had gone by. Rather than get mad, I embraced it. These became the credo of our office—our new guiding principles.

The first one was, "Always take the high road. Do the right thing." This was my instruction to everyone, and I told them that if they ever saw me hesitate, to take me aside and remind me again of my values (after all, I'm only human and I make mistakes). I decided a long time ago that I would "warranty" my dental work for five years. This meant that if something went wrong with a restoration (not including root canals, perio issues, etc.), I would ask for forgiveness from the patient and redo my work at no charge. I feel that if a margin is not sealed (seen on an x-ray at a later time), a contact opens, porcelain chips, the patient isn't happy with the color (even if they approved the color before delivery), or anything that the patient feels isn't right, I'll make it right. The financial coordinator and the scheduler know this and don't ask me anymore if the patient should be charged.

In addition to a five-year replacement agreement, I included a golden rule codicil to my "do the right thing" motto. I would put myself in the patient's shoes and try to imagine how I would feel under a similar circumstance. An example would be insurance coverage. If a patient had the same insurance for longer than a year, we should know most of its limitations. If the insurance covered a prophylaxis once every six months and we did one a day too soon, we should cover the cost of the cleaning. If we miscalculated the maximum coverage because the patient saw a specialist at _our_ request and then needed more treatment, who's fault is it?

"Do the right thing" doesn't always pertain to money issues (although those are the most prevalent). A phone call to a patient who had a rough time in the chair, or a note to someone who lost a family member doesn't cost you anything. Smoothing a very slightly chipped tooth also shouldn't be a profit opportunity. In all, "Do the right thing" is something that helps you sleep at night.

The second value for the office is an adaptation of a Maya Angelou quote, "People won't remember what you said or did, but they will remember how you made them feel." A welcoming smile, a compliment, and a hand on the shoulder during an injection are all acts of kindness that we forget to do on a regular basis. When a patient hasn't been in for a long time, why do we ask why they haven't been in? It immediately puts them on the defensive and they may not realize it right away, but they won't feel great about coming in to see us again. Why not say, "We are so glad you've come in. Is there anything specific you'd like us to examine or is this just a check-up?" There are times when patients refuse to swallow their own saliva (I call this TSS or toxic saliva syndrome) or when they need to stop biting you. There is no way you can convince them otherwise, and if you try, you'll get angry patients who will remember that you yelled at them. "You can't teach a pig to fly. It's aerodynamically impossible and it angers the pig." (This might be an unofficial fourth motto).

I have worked with many hygienists who are proud of their work, and they should be, but some take it a little too far. When a patient doesn't do "what they were instructed to do" the very proud hygienist gets frustrated that the patient didn't understand the importance of their homework. When the discussion gets around to home care before the next appointment, using words like "you need to" or a head tilt with an upraised eyebrow—which essentially says, "you better understand because I'm tired of..."—you are insuring that the patient will remember how you made them feel.

The last value is that we always "Under promise and overdeliver." This is probably the most frequent concept that we endeavor to pursue. A few examples include the following:

1. When scheduling, tell the patient that the procedure will take longer than you actually think. It makes you look more efficient, and you can congratulate the patient for being so good that the procedure went smoothly. If you run into snags and it does take longer, you've already set the expectations properly.

2. When doing an exam (either a first time comprehensive, periodic, or emergency) and it's necessary to give a price quote, estimate higher than normal, but say you aren't absolutely sure of the exact amount. However, the financial coordinator (or office manager or scheduler), will give you a more exact fee. The expectations are that the cost is $2,000, and when they're told it is $1,853 there is a little moment of happiness. Do the same for insurance benefits if it's an unknown plan.

3. Before giving an injection, let them know that you will do your best, but these always hurt just a little. Give a full three minutes of a topical, then give a three second injection, pull the syringe out and wait another ten seconds. Then give your injection slowly. It will be about as painless as possible and the patient, who was expecting pain will be happy that it went well.

My first job at age sixteen was scooping ice cream for a national franchise. My training included practicing scooping up exactly two and a half ounces, and it took a few hours until the scoops were predictably accurate. But before I was allowed to scoop for the public, I was told to scoop the exact amount into the cone, to weigh it by peering hard at the cone and moving it slightly up and down a few times, and then to add just a little more. The buyers felt like they were getting more for their dollar.

We can do the same. When we see an emergency patient and merely talk or do something that takes a very short time, why can't we do it at no charge? It fulfills all three of the values: we make someone feel good, we give them more than they expected, and we do the right thing.

One last note. When creating values, mottos, or credos, they must be completely and fully embraced by the leader(s), or they are just words. ENRON was an energy company based in Houston, and their corporate slogan was "Integrity." In the early 2000's, it was discovered that they had committed massive corporate fraud resulting in arrests from the top down. For the corporate board of ENRON, integrity was a jumble of nine letters with no meaning.

My mission statement didn't work the way it was intended. We thought our patients would be impressed by what we *told* them. Even though we were trying to live up to those statements, no one seemed to notice. It was a fun team building exercise and I felt we came together in our belief's, but our assumptions were wrong. Just because it was written down didn't mean it was true. The reason the guiding principles worked is because we lived them every day, we reaffirmed them every day, and we believed them to be authentic. The sayings weren't all about how you should treat your patients, they were all about how you should treat people. Please feel free to use them; they will enhance any practice that does.

Quick – Slick Back Your Hair. Here Comes a Customer. It's Time to Sell a Condo.

CHAPTER TWELVE

I hope this doesn't happen in your office:

"You need a crown Mrs. Knicklesqueezer," said Dr. Bigboat, confidently and with a big smile.

"How much is it?" asked Mrs. Knicklesqueezer tentatively.

"Well, I'll let the little lady at the front desk go through that with you."

-Change scenes to the front desk.-

"I see Dr. Bigboat has diagnosed a crown," said the front-desk scheduler. "When would you like to schedule that appointment, Mrs. Knicklesqueezer?"

"How much is the crown?" she asked again. This time a little more forcibly.

"It's one thousand, seven hundred and fifty-two," the scheduler said proudly. She had just been to a seminar where they said never to mention the word "dollar" when giving a quote.

"Gadzooks! that's a lot of money." exclaimed Mrs. Knicklesqueezer.

"Well, there is a lot of time involved and the lab costs a lot of money. And the assistant is one of the highest paid—she's that good." (*Might as well get in a little promotion for my best friend, the scheduler thinks. Maybe she'll buy me a gift once she hears about me complimenting her.*) "Dr. Bigboat only uses the best materials, and this is a high-rent area, so everyone here charges a lot." (*Oops, maybe I shouldn't have said that last part*). The little scheduler obviously never took the course that discussed how you never defend fees.

"Why do I need a crown in the first place?" asked Mrs. Knicklesqueezer.

"Well, um…because Dr. Bigboat recommended it." Inspiration hit at the last second and the scheduler was proud of her answer.

"Well, um, I'll let you know what I decide." Mrs. Knicklesqueezer walked out and never called back.

"What just happened?" asked the little scheduler at the front desk.

What just happened was that no one in the office understood sales. The above scenario was very similar to my experiences in the beginning of working in my own office. Maybe not that bad, but definitely not very good. I would recommend treatment and sometimes the patients would proceed, but sometimes they wouldn't. I was told to be more confident. But when I was more confident, I was told I was arrogant. One of my patients in my first office (the white elephant office) left the practice and I never knew why. Later she went to the office I ended up purchasing. When she saw me at the new office, her face told it all. "Why are you here?" she asked. "Honestly, I left the old office because of your arrogance." The good news was that we ended up working it out. She's really nice and still a patient today. But that didn't help my closing skills back then when I needed more help.

I had heard I should do some analysis and figure out what my closure rate was. These were the patients who actually did the treatment I recommended. I went back in the schedule about four years and looked up every new patient. I totaled the dollar amount diagnosed and then totaled the dollar amount completed after one year. Going back four years gave me three years of data. My percentage rate for those years was somewhere around thirty percent. Even *I* knew that wasn't very good.

Seminars in case-presentation helped me a lot, and the whole office learned how to be better in that regard. A key point was to create value before telling the cost. When you do it in reverse, the cost stands out, blocking all rational thought.

"Hello, I'm looking for a very nice used car," said the buyer.

"Well, that's just wonderful. This baby you're looking at has a sticker price of $52,498.00. Would you like to buy it?"

I've already mentioned this twice in previous chapters, but it's so very important. There's a formula we now use on every diagnosis and suggested treatment plan. The plan creates value to the extent that cost is no longer the driving factor for acceptance. It seems obvious, but it does take a while to make it a habit. It's important to spotlight the value in every discussion before mentioning cost. In order for this to work, and for you to sleep at night, you have to be ethical in your diagnosis since this is for needed dentistry only (this does not work for strictly cosmetic cases). The three-level technique is as follows:

1. Describe the problem. Use intra-oral photos and/or x-rays whenever possible.

2. Describe what will or could happen if nothing was done. The more involved you get in this description, the better.

3. Describe the treatment options.

Now let's look at an example of this process at work:

Step one: "Mr. Caramel, you have decay on your upper right first molar. It's the one that is second from the back. There is a very large silver filling on the biting surface connecting to both the front and back of the tooth. There is a crack in the filling in almost the very middle, as you can see on the intra-oral photo. The shadowy dark area with the brownish tint on either side of the crack is decay and it's quite large. "

Step two: "If you do nothing that crack will grow, and the decay will get much bigger. The decay now lines most of the filling and it's protected from your toothbrush and toothpaste because of the filling. Mouthwash might get in about a millimeter, but the decay goes much deeper than that. Left alone, the decay will grow down towards the nerve and outward towards the side of the tooth. There is now a race between which will happen first. Will you need root canal therapy or will the tooth fracture? If it fractures, we might be able to save the tooth, but there are no promises."

Step three: "If we can get to this tooth in a timely manner, we can remove the old filling, remove the decay, bulk the tooth up with a medicated, hard impact resin and then place a crown. There are no guarantees that you won't need a root canal, but the sooner you get to it, the better the odds will be that you'll be able to avoid it. We could also extract this tooth and discuss its replacement, but I think that's a bit premature for now."

Another example:

Step one: "Mr. Icecracker, the reason you're catching food between your teeth on that lower left area is you've broken a piece of tooth where two teeth meet. You can see it easily on this x-ray."

Step Two: "If you do nothing, many things will happen. The tooth behind the gap will move forward and try to close the gap, making a gap behind that tooth and so forth. This movement is a tilting one. The back teeth will lean forward towards its contact with the next tooth, which means your bite will get messed up as the teeth lean in towards the front of your mouth. Another thing is that whenever you catch food between your teeth, which is now a certainty, your body treats it as an infection. Most of the time you can get it out by swishing, flossing, and brushing, but when you leave some behind, the gums don't like it. The infection of the bacteria on the food causes your body to fight it with an inflammatory response, and the gums and bone become the battleground. In addition to changing your bite and creating a periodontal problem, the missing part of the tooth has now exposed the underlying dentin. The enamel coating is gone in this area, so now decay can penetrate the tooth much easier."

Step three: "If we can get to this tooth in a timely manner, we can repair the damage with a strong resin filling that will bond to your tooth. The contact will be restored, and the dentin will be covered."

Practice this showing-value process with your everyday diagnoses and it will become a habit. Whenever a patient walks out without an appointment, look back to see if you created the value necessary to proceed.

Hey, I Could Use a Hand Here

CHAPTER THIRTEEN

It was one of those days. There are all kinds of them, but this was one where I didn't have enough time to give that little extra boost that would ensure the patient would schedule for a needed crown. My schedule was fairly well planned, but you can't anticipate when a patient says, "While you are doing that filling, can you check the one next to it? I think I broke it while eating last night." Of course, it needed treatment and the patient wanted it right then, so you run a touch late and try to make up for it when you can. I tried to make up time when I was doing a prophy check and the patient needed a crown. As soon as I left the room, I heard the patient ask the hygienist, "Do I really need a crown?" I wasn't thrilled with her answer.

"Umm, well, sure," answered Lisa the hygienist.

"You really don't sound sure," commented Sammy Skeptical.

"Uh, I've only been here two years and I don't know that kinda stuff," she defended herself.

Needless to say, the patient did not schedule for the restorative appointment.

Employees fall into all sorts of categories. Some are good workers, some are self-starters, and some are empathetic. Sometimes you get one that hits all the "greats," but one asset that is essential is the employee that helps you with sales. Up to this point in my career, I hadn't really put any emphasis on this because I really thought it was *my* job. I liked it when the hygienists spoke up about needed treatment, but we never trained for it. I had a few moments of pleasure when I heard one of my assistants mirroring my sales technique while walking by the operatory on the same day that the hygienist had failed. I was so proud, I could've bought a spittoon and spit in it. I didn't realize I needed help, but once I heard it, I started interviewing for it.

I hope the above hygienist scenario doesn't happen in your office, but the question really does get asked of your staff more often than you think. The answer that they give can either be the one that loses the patient or the one that convinces them that they are in the right spot. Any hesitation, looking around, or neutral answers by your staff member gives a signal to your patient that perhaps they are with the wrong dentist. On the other hand, a confident answer will solidify the patient's resolve to proceed. Please remember that this is for needed dentistry only and the dentist must be ethical. If the dentist is over diagnosing, the staff realizes it quickly, and the sideways glances start up. However, if you have the respect of your staff, the conversation will go like this:

"Ugh! I really don't want another crown. Do I really need one?" asked Donny Doubtful.

"It's obvious that there is decay on the side of that large filling. As Dr. Disraeli mentioned, if you do nothing the decay will get bigger and will cause other problems. I know it's no fun getting dental work, but the earlier you get it done, the easier the procedure will be. You're going to be fine. Dr. Disraeli is very good at this," answered Stacy Smiler.

How about the cosmetic or aesthetic case? It's not essential dentistry, so the questions from the patient are different. But no matter what the questions are, the staff member has to assure the patient that they are in the right hands by saying things like:

"Dr. Disraeli is really very good at this."

"I've worked on many cases with Dr. Disraeli, and I know you'll be happy with the final result."

"Dr. Disraeli is very careful and methodical. There are a lot of steps needed to make this perfect and Dr. D. never rushes them."

"I've worked with Dr. Disraeli on a lot of cosmetic cases, and I can assure you that he will not only listen to you, but he will also answer questions you hadn't yet thought to ask."

It's important to train your staff how you would like them to respond to this very common situation. This is a two-party sale in which, two individuals tell the buyer the same thing. One is the dentist and the other a staff member. It seems like the patient would assume that the staff member was just stating the party line, but patients almost always see the staff member as an honest, individual giving their own opinion.

A different kind of two-party sale is a proactive one (versus the above reactive one). It's one in which a staff member actually starts the conversation about producing dentistry.

Usually, the proactive employee is the hygienist. Hygienists are not allowed to diagnose dentistry, but that doesn't mean they can't bring noticeable problems to the attention of the dentist. Before the hygienist mentions the issue to the dentist, there's usually plenty of time to explain what was seen to the patient.

"Mrs. Sparkletooth, while cleaning your teeth, I could see a dark line up against an existing filling," mentioned Sandy Scraper, the hygienist. "There's a shadowy halo around it that usually indicates decay, and it looks like it extends a little further than I like. I'm going to ask Dr. Disraeli to take a look and see if it's a problem or nothing at all." Nowhere in this conversation was there an absolute statement or diagnosis, so Sandy was legally and ethically covered. "The filling is fairly large to begin with and if that dark coloring is decay, it could end up with you needing a crown. Dr. Disraeli will be in for the exam, and we'll ask him to take a look."

And then a few minutes later, "Hello, Mrs. Sparkletooth, how are you today?" asked Dr. Disraeli.

She looked sideways at her hygienist, "Fine, I guess."

Sandy interrupted easily, "Dr. Disraeli, Mrs. Sparkletooth is a great patient. She takes very good care of her teeth." A compliment is always in order. "But during your exam, would you mind paying special attention to tooth #19? There is a dark line next to the filling and perhaps a shadow next to that. I told Mrs. Sparkletooth that the existing filling was quite large, and I was a little worried." Sandy has now told Dr. Disraeli that there was a discussion about the tooth. If he ignores her or throws her under a bus by saying, "It's nothing," then she'll never mention any potential issues again. And rightfully so.

"Ah, I see what you mean, Sandy. You've got great vision. That's a difficult area to see." Now no matter what Dr. D. says, Sandy feels validated, and Mrs. Sparkletooth starts to trust Sandy a bit more.

Mrs. Sparkletooth had a real problem. It wasn't made up or exaggerated. Sandy noticed and said something. She wasn't pushy or hesitant. She made sure Dr. Disraeli saw it as well. He checked it out and then went through the normal three-step sales procedure. Mrs. Sparkletooth listened to Dr. Disraeli perhaps a little more than normal because Sandy saw it first and Dr. Disraeli agreed with Sandy. This two-party sales technique isn't unethical, immoral, or wrong in any way. Patients are often hesitant to do what's right for them for many reasons. If we can convince them to do what really does need to be done, are we not doing them a valuable service?

For aesthetic cases, your staff can still be proactive and more of the staff can get involved. When they see a patient with stained or crooked or malformed teeth, it's very easy to ask generic questions leading towards aesthetic dentistry. It's important that you don't come across as judgmental or too pushy.

"Ms. Trashtooth, your teeth are in dire need of cosmetic dentistry," said Reba Rookie. She had heard Dr. Disraeli mention that he wanted to do more cosmetic cases and she wanted to help. "Dr. Disraeli is really good at that kind of stuff," obviously, forgetting her nomenclature class.

"Well!" Ms. Trashtooth huffed. "I just spent $15,000 getting them done last year in Beverly Hills, and they look great," she said hesitantly.

Reba thinks, *Don't say anything. Don't say anything. Don't say anything… can't help myself.* "Wow, you got ripped off," Reba exclaimed.

A better way to light the fires towards cosmetic dentistry would be to ask a more open-ended question. I took a class right around the time I started doing more cases and the lecturer said she always asked the same question to every new patient, "Are you satisfied with the appearance of your teeth?" This is an okay question to ask, and when I asked it on the first visit, ninety-nine percent of the time the answer was "yes." The answer was usually said with no inflection, softly, and confidently. I realized years later after I stopped asking that question, that I had not established enough trust to get an honest answer. It took going to another seminar for it to sink in.

The next lecturer explained that cosmetic dentistry was something that most patients wanted to some degree, (remember the explosion of whitening products?) but were afraid of the result after seeing so many friends with black lines at the gumline of their obvious and highly opaque crowns. Money was a concern, but more of a concern was "What would I look like?" The lecturer went on to say that having a beautifully photographed book on previous cases that you have done will ease that fear. He also mentioned that you can only see the ugly crowns. The ones that fit in perfectly are never noticed, so show them what you can do. His next topic was an improvement on the "Are you satisfied with the appearance of your teeth?" question. His suggestion was to take it one step further. "If you had a magic wand, would you change anything in your smile?"

I tried the above method for a while. The photo album took some time to put together, but it became a primary tool in having patients desiring cosmetic work. Unfortunately, I found that the magic wand question was still too weak…so I changed it to, "If you had a magic wand, what would you change about your teeth?" The difference was the word, "What." It forces the patient to think of something rather than just opting out of the discussion. My wife heard a cousin on the East Coast say that she was asked by her cosmetic dentist, "What do you love about your smile?" which is also a great open-ended question. If the answer was still, "I'm very satisfied with my teeth," tell them, "That's great," and move on. However, any positive response opens a dialogue and gives you a chance to strut your stuff. Most patients won't make a cosmetic decision on the first day based on your recommendation. But they did hear you and you planted a seed. The next time they come in, figure out a way to bring it up again, but very gently. Until they tell you, "I'm not interested," discuss it sporadically. I have had patients get the work done ten years after I first mentioned it.

And because the theme of this chapter is two-party sales, teach your team how to start the cosmetic conversation. In fact, teach them all about two-party sales so that it's an easy conversational direction for everyone.

She Stole *HOW* Much?

CHAPTER FOURTEEN

Life was good. The stars came out at night and the sun shone during the day. I was at the point where I felt that the systems were in place, and I could relax just a little. Oops!

I had a patient who liked to pay in cash. He had come in the day before and had paid his normal way. The total was about $800, but it was a very busy day, and I didn't remember to look for the cash. I should never have had to look, but honesty for some people is a thin veneer waiting for a tiny crack. The next day a patient paid with cash, and I was handed the cash in the approved way, which struck a spark/reminder about the previous days cash patient.

I was feeling a little lazy, so instead of looking at the printed day-sheet (yes, we printed everything then), I went to the software program and looked up the patient's account. It showed that he had paid the complete amount, and like usual, he had paid in cash. My heart skipped a beat because I had seen no cash. I then went to the digital day sheet and saw that there were two day-sheets for the previous day. My heart had now skipped two beats and I was hoping I could get it started again. The one that I had seen, which had almost all but two of the patients listed, did not show the cash patient as having paid in cash, check, or credit card. The other day-sheet had the cash patient listed, as well as another cash patient for $1,500 (this patient had come in to settle his bill but had had no dental work done that day). This day-sheet showed them both paying in cash. I had deposited no cash, so where was the $2,300? It was after work, so I decided to do a little detective work and went back to the reports section of my software and found a lot more double day-sheets from several years with a total of about $50,000.

I called my attorney who called in a private investigator. I then contacted a forensic accountant and my insurance company. It was indisputable, my office manager of over fifteen years had stolen money. My insurance company paid $17,000 and I ate the rest.

So...what's the lesson? Do everything you can to avoid being embezzled. Check your day-sheets against the schedule every day before you leave. You will be surprised at the number of simple mistakes that come up. We are all human and we all make mistakes, and it takes just a little work to check. Imagine a patient "accidentally" getting billed for two cleanings on the same day. It definitely happens! When they get the bill, they'll wonder how many other people you double charged. What about the x-rays that weren't done because the patient was newly pregnant, but was charged because the scheduler didn't know about the pregnancy and lazily just followed the schedule? What will she think when she gets the bill and knows without a doubt that she did not get x-rays? On the other hand, can you call a patient to ask for more money when after doing your daily audit, you discover only two of the three fillings were posted? You will not look more efficient if you are error free, but if you do make mistakes, you'll look sloppy at the very least and criminal at worst.

So, what happened with my embezzler? When all was in absolute order, my attorney asked me if I was ready to turn it over to the police. I asked him if it would be appropriate to write her a letter and ask for the money back. He said, "It couldn't hurt." Famous last words.

We received a letter from her attorney three days later explaining we had it all wrong. I was the one at fault for stealing the money from myself to make the sale of my business more lucrative (I really didn't understand the logic), I was committing insurance fraud with her as the patsy (she was the one controlling all aspects of the insurance billing), and I was sexually harassing her (which I wasn't). I asked my attorney for advice. He told me that her counter-aggression was a normal tactic when trying to avoid prosecution. It would be very easy to win in court. I asked him how much it would cost, and he said about the same amount that had been embezzled.

My choices were to let it go or attack her in court and have the stink of scandal riding over me for the rest of my career with no monetary gain. Revenge with a penalty or turn the other cheek. Please don't judge me, but I chose to do nothing. Well, almost nothing. I'm warning you to be careful. Try not to let yourself get put into a position where you have to defend yourself. Spend the necessary time and keep watch over your practice. It's your business, so act like it!

In summary:

1. Check your day sheets against the schedule every day.

2. Check all adjustments to see if they are legitimate.

3. Check that yesterday's month-to-date plus today's deposit equals today's month-to-date.

4. Call your software company for tips. I found out that mine could generate a very simple report that listed the date of every day sheet created during the reported time. I now check mine every month to make sure there are no duplicates and no weekend day sheets.

I Have Only One Story Dammit! Give Me a Handoff!

CHAPTER FIFTEEN

"Dr. Givahoot's office. Watcha need?" asked Betty Lou.

"Uh, this is Jane Plane. I'm an existing patient of Dr. Givahoot's and I broke a tooth a few weeks ago while I was on vacation, and it's starting to hurt. It's on the upper right and I think it's a molar."

"Okay, Jane. Why don't ya come in tomorrow at two."

"I'll be there."

The next day, Jane came in. "Kin I help yoo?" asked Betty Lou.

"I'm Jane Plane. I have a two o'clock appointment."

"Right. What was it for again?"

"I broke a tooth while on vacation."

"Is it hurting you?"

"Yes." Jane was starting to get frustrated.

"Where is the pain?"

Jane sighed, "It's on the upper right towards the rear."

"Okay then. Wanda Mae will be with ya shortly," Betty Lou smiled.

Twenty minutes went by and finally Wanda Mae came out to the waiting room and in a very loud voice announced, "Is Jane Plane here? Jane Plane?"

Jane stood up, looked around and saw no one else in the room. She walked with Wanda Mae back to the operatory. "So, why're ya here?" asked Wanda Mae.

Jane went through the whole scenario once again, trying to say everything to speed things up. Wanda Mae left to get Dr. Givahoot.

"Hello, I'm Dr. Givahoot. You must be Jane. What seems to be the problem?

"Dr. Givahoot, I'm an existing patient. I've been seeing you for about five years."

"Oh, then. Well, it's nice to see you again. Why are you here?"

Jane went through it all again and was starting to wonder why she continued to see Dr. Givahoot. An x-ray was taken, and an exam was given. The treatment recommended was a root canal, build-up, and an all-porcelain crown for tooth #3. "Go on up to the front and Betty Lou will take care of you," said Dr. Givahoot.

Jane found her way back to the front desk and waited for Betty Lou to acknowledge her. It took a few minutes. "Watcha need, honey?"

"Dr. Givahoot wants to do some treatment on my upper tooth," Jane answered, having a bad feeling about what was to come next.

"Well? What did he want to do?"

Jane had almost had enough. "Why don't you go find someone to tell you. That's not my job. I don't know how to tell you the dental terms, and I'm tired of repeating myself."

"Well, you don't have to get nasty about it. I was only asking."

Jane had now had enough, "Well, now I'm only asking you to send my x-rays to the email that you have on file for me."

Ouch! I'm certain that your office is nowhere near this bad, but are there some elements in this scenario that made you cringe? If you want to be a highly professional office, you not only have to recognize the problems, but also figure out a way to solve them. The above scenario is bad in so many ways, but there are only two main issues I want to address. I believe that once those are solved, the other minor issues will take care of themselves.

The most frustrating thing for Jane was that she had to explain her problems multiple times. It seemed to her that everyone was simply curious, but not polite enough to tell the next person in line. She had to tell her story four times, and that included telling Betty Lou twice. Betty Lou was lazy and couldn't be bothered writing down Jane's problem, and by the time twenty-four hours had gone by, Betty Lou didn't even pretend to know any of Jane's story. By the time Jane told her story to Dr. Givahoot, Jane had it memorized.

How do you think Jane would have felt if Betty Lou not only recognized her as she came in, but also said something like, "Don't worry Jane, Dr. G. will take a real close look at that broken upper right molar. Other than that, how was your vacation?" Jane would have instantly felt like she was in the right place and would be taken care of properly.

The next step would be Betty Lou's responsibility. She would need to inform Wanda Mae everything that Jane had described. Wanda Mae would then need to let Jane know, subtly, that she had knowledge of Jane's problem. The passing of information is extremely important, but only if it is used properly. It would actually be more time efficient if Betty Lou told the whole office the story in the morning meeting. And if there were any changes when Jane came in, Betty Lou could add another chapter.

Now it's Wanda Mae's turn. As they were walking down the hall to the operatory, "I hear that you had an unexpected glitch while you were in Hawaii, Jane. Other than that, how was your vacation?" And then once they were in the room, "Tell me a little of the background of your broken molar. It's on the upper right, isn't it?" Then Wanda Mae listens actively, asking appropriate questions and taking notes. Wanda Mae now needs to tell Dr. Givahoot.

Wanda Mae can discuss the issue in front of the patient or give Dr. Givahoot all the info out of earshot of the patient. When it's given in front of the patient, the assistant can ask, "Did I get that right, Jane?" This gives the patient a chance to add to the story. Everyone is on board. If the story is told behind the scenes, the dentist recaps in front of the patient and asks, "Did I get that right, Jane?" The only difference is that in the second scenario, the dentist spends more face-to-face time with the patient. But sometimes we don't have the luxury of time.

So now Jane has told her story once and everyone is in the loop. Dr. Givahoot does the exam and remembering Chapter Twelve, goes through the "sales" progression (1. Diagnosis; 2. What will happen if nothing is done;

3. Treatment options). He and Wanda Mae stay with Jane until there are no more dental questions. "Betty Lou can help you with all of your insurance, financial, and scheduling questions. And if you have any more dental questions, just have Betty Lou call me over," said Dr. Givahoot with a kindly smile.

Telling the story once was the first of the problems in the bad example, but the second problem ties in to the first. In the bad example, Jane was left alone after the exam to not only locate the front desk, but to then explain what was needed. That's a big responsibility and not fair to Jane. What happens if she makes a mistake? Would they do a root canal on the wrong tooth? Would she be charged more if she forgot to mention one of the procedures?

The same rule of telling the story once also works on the reverse side. Dr. Givahoot and Jane decided on a course of action. Wanda Mae was there and now walks with Jane to the scheduler, Betty Lou. In a very professional yet kind office, there is a handoff whenever the next staff member takes over. At a minimum, the patient's name is used and something nice is said. A description of what has happened and what will happen is next if it's appropriate. This happened to Jane on the way into the exam room. Her name was used every step of the way and because of that, Jane knew that she was more than just a broken tooth. Her story was described, and Jane knew that they understood her issues. Talking about what will happen next was not yet appropriate, so it wasn't discussed. However, it all comes together and full circle when Jane returns to Betty Lou to discuss the next visit. At this stage, there are five steps we need to take. They are all done facing the next staff member, but the comments are actually directed towards the patient.

1. Use the patient's name. Everyone likes to know that they aren't just a tooth or a procedure.

2. Make sure there is a compliment directed towards the patient somewhere in the handoff. Remember that people *will* remember how you made them feel.

3. Discuss what was done in as much detail as possible. This is so that the patient recognizes all you have done and when fees are discussed, will sense the value in it. Give as much information as you can and definitely include the nonchargeable items like a toothbrush, cancer screening, or oral hygiene instructions.

4. Describe what happens next. In a hygiene recall visit, it's simply the interval timing of the next visit and extras as needed like x-rays, probing, or intra-oral photos. If the next visit is a restorative visit, give lots of information, even though everything the scheduler/ financial officer needs has already been placed in the computer. The patient needs to hear all of it while checking out to make sure it's accurate and to create as much value as possible.

5. Next is the diplomatic step. The assistant, hygienist, or even dentist in some offices, smiles and says goodbye. If the patient responds with a compliment (because we complimented them first), the staff member says thank you and then gently asks for a referral or an online review. It can be very natural if you practice, and you *should* practice. We all need the reviews and new patients.

"Hi, Betty Lou. Jane is all done for today. She did incredibly well. It was a long visit, and she did everything we asked of her." Wanda Mae was facing Betty Lou but kept Jane in her peripheral vision. "We did everything we planned for today's visit. Dr. Givahoot removed all the old restoration and decay and then built the tooth back up, creating a more even thickness for the crown. The tooth was then fine-tuned, and an impression and bite check were taken. The temporary was made, polished, cemented, and cleaned. And here we are." Wanda Mae smiled at Betty Lou and then turned and smiled at Jane. "Thank you again, Jane. You made our job today very easy." Wanda Mae turned back towards Betty Lou, "Our next visit will be to deliver the crown we prepared today." She turned back towards Jane, "Don't forget to let us know if you have any issues with the temporary. We are only a phone call away."

Jane seemed very happy. "You know, it went a lot easier than I thought it would. I was really comfortable the entire time. You are all very professional."

"We definitely appreciate the complement. If there is any way you can write an online review, we would appreciate it greatly. Most patients find their new dentists that way if they're new to town."

"I would love to," replies Jane sincerely.

The office manager is always on the lookout for reviews and when one comes in, the dentist is notified so an online thank-you can be made, as well as letting the patient know everyone in the office is grateful.

Okay. It's actually one story told many times and multiple handoffs done the same way. The patient feels good because they know they were listened to and treated in a caring and respectful way. The dental staff feels good because they have taken care of a grateful patient and there is a definite feeling of accomplishment in a job well done. The dentist feels good because the team-work feels authentic and micromanagement supervision isn't necessary.

Why, Why, Why
Do I Need a Morning Meeting?

CHAPTER SIXTEEN

There are a lot of nonbeliever dentists who run late. And as they throw their car keys onto their desk, grab a lab coat, loupes, and a mask, and haul ass into the operatory where the patient has been sitting for a long fifteen minutes, a dust cloud follows them in. As nonchalantly as possible, the dentist says, "And how are you today... um, er...!" The unprepared assistant mouths the patient's name with exaggeration to the dentist. And then the dentist blurts out, "SUE!"

The arrogant dentist misunderstands and blows a kiss back at the assistant.

Of course, a prepared assistant would have written the name in large block letters. What an enabler! There is no way to get an always-delayed dentist to get into the office early (or even on time), so if this is you and you have no intention of changing, skip to the next chapter.

The hardest part about a morning meeting is that it cuts into your bank account. Either you are using up valuable production time or paying overtime for your staff. Have you heard about the contest between two lumberjacks where one stops frequently to sharpen his axe and the other one is much more productive...in the beginning? Of course, the sharpening allows for less fatigue and faster cutting. Which means the lumberjack who stops to sharpen his axe cuts more logs. The morning meeting is the same.

When I first started practicing, the morning meeting was for those dentists who always tried new things and threw out ninety percent of them over time. I didn't want to have that reputation. In my first office, I heard it said that morning meetings were a complete waste of time, "I know who my patients are and what they need. Why should I talk about it?" I didn't disagree, but then, I also didn't realize how badly run the office was. And by the way, this is where I heard the stories about the ninety percent thing. I was being taught how to be an old geezer dentist while still in my twenties. "Why, I oughta…"

The morning meeting is a time to get everyone on the same page. As your staff trickles in and starts brief conversations about their lives while they get their lab coats and put away their personal items, some might be harried and others might be sleepy. One might have a sick spouse and another might have just seen a great movie. The gossip could go on forever, and it's helpful for the group to connect about their outside lives, but the morning meeting becomes the trigger that brings your staff together in the office. Everyone knows what's needed and what's expected. By habit, everyone chooses the same chair or area. Almost in unison, everyone looks toward the leader of the meeting as soon as a greeting with a smile is offered. This is the most important part; the absolute readiness and eagerness to start the day. Everyone has a schedule and is looking for the things that concern them.

The morning meeting should have a revolving leader. Each week, a different staff member leads the meeting, inserting their own personality and point of view. This will keep the meetings fresher and more interesting as well as making each staff member feel more like a part of the team. If possible, the morning leader should go through the schedule ahead of everyone else to look for bottlenecks and places for emergencies.

In a fifteen-minute morning meeting you need at least twenty minutes. Each person should go through their own responsibility in the schedule and check the need for x-rays (full set or periodic and frequency) and prophy exams, as well as verify the treatments being done that day. You should also check to see if there is anything outstanding on each treatment plan. Are there health issues we should be aware of? Are there personality quirks? This pre-meeting can be done anytime and anywhere there is a free computer, but the actual meeting needs to be on time and with the group. If you start earlier than your normal eight hours, be prepared to pay time and a half. You will get far more than what you pay. It will also help if you have tablet computers so that everyone can be up to and beyond wherever the leader is at that time.

The leader of the week should start the meeting with a smile and a discussion of the first patient of the day. I usually start in the first chair on the schedule that's in the upper left and move through all the patients at the same time. Then, obviously, I move down to the next time a patient is coming in. Don't forget to encourage stories about the patients, as it will not only help you remember them better, but it might give you something more to bring up during their visit as well, which helps tie them into your specific office. It also makes your patients more interesting and will keep you from getting bored or burned out.

"All right everyone, let's get started. Patient X is coming in for a prophy."

"Patient X has a latex allergy; patient Y needs a premed."

"Why does she need a premed?" asked a newer employee.

"Let me look. Hmm, it was for a mitral valve prolapse. Wait, the protocol has changed, and she no longer needs antibiotics. Okay, let's change her chart and let her know."

"Is patient A pregnant? If so, we can schedule her x-rays for after she gives birth."

"Unfortunately, I heard that she lost the baby."

"Okay, is this one where we acknowledge the loss or leave her alone? Who knows her best?"

"Patient B is getting a crown. This is November and I'm pretty sure he had gum surgery six months ago from someone we don't normally refer. Does he still have insurance left? Can we wait two months to do this to start with renewed insurance?"

"I checked when I made the appointment. We're good."

Or…"I'll check on the insurance, then I'll call him as soon as I find out if he has to pay out-of-pocket and if his insurance resets January 1 or another time. I'll give him the option of rescheduling for next year."

"Patient C likes to hold her own suction," said the hygienist to the assistant. The schedule was for a filling.

"Patient D's birthday is today. Does he like attention? Can we all sing to him when he walks in? Or is he more the stoic type, in which case we can quietly wish him a happy birthday one at a time?"

"Patient E is getting a crown delivery today. Just as a reminder, her temp came off while we were on vacation. Dr. Helpsalot took care of recementing it and didn't charge her. But he did say her sensitivity was a little higher than it should be. Let's make sure we acknowledge this so she knows we are in touch with Dr. H., and we can possibly set her expectations regarding a root canal."

"Patient F is doing a metal try-in for his new partial. Let's make sure we remind him that delivery day is just the first of several possible appointments for adjusting. Remember, underpromise and overdeliver."

"Okay everyone. That's it. Let's get started, and remember, have a great day!"

I have been doing a morning meeting for most of my career. In the beginning, they were shorter because I had fewer patients. As my practice grew, the information shared during the morning meeting also grew in importance. We were all very good at writing notes and since I don't have a photographic memory, these notes enabled us to treat every patient with a high degree of attention. We were able to look our patients in the eye and make them feel special. They felt like people who mattered, and not like just some patient number on a chart.

I Love My Specialists!

CHAPTER SEVENTEEN

I was having one of those days. We were a little overbooked and since it was Monday, I was also getting some emergencies. I over polished a contact on a cranky patient and had to explain how I wouldn't be able to deliver it that day. I didn't have a CADCAM or an oven, so I had to try to find something positive to say. "I guess I'm too much of a perfectionist, Mr. Frownface. The crown isn't exactly what I want, so I'm going to send it back to the lab so they can make this an A-plus restoration."

"Hogwash. You messed it up, and now I have to pay the price. What are you gonna do to make it up to me?"

While I negotiated a settlement that would make Old Man Frownface happy, my assistant said she needed to go home. She had a headache and wasn't feeling well. Earlier, my hygienist said that the two of them drank the night before while celebrating her birthday. To top it off, a cosmetic patient, whose case I had finished a week earlier, was coming in to complain that her newly crowned teeth were too short. She had worn temporaries for two months and finally agreed that they represented the exact look she wanted. It was one of those moments that made me question my career (even if only for a few seconds).

After lunch (fortunately, I was out of tequila), I was scheduled to do a crown on a rear molar that a new endodontist had worked on. He had done the buildup, so my job was going to be fairly easy, and I was looking forward to it. "Before we get started, I wanted to tell you what the root canal guy said to me about you," my patient told me after saying hello. My heart started to sink. How much more can a guy handle? Would it be ethical to send out my hungover dental assistant to go buy the industrial size Don Julio Silver?

"He said I was very lucky to have found you. You are one of the best dentists he has ever worked with. How much did you pay him?" I was stunned. Considering my day so far, this was the exact opposite of what I expected. "I don't pay him anything. I just give him a gift certificate to the candy store, and I follow him around with a camera for blackmail reasons." We both laughed, but a smile stayed with me for the rest of the day.

Over the next few months, all of my endo referrals came back with a similar story. My head started to swell. My peers thought I was really good. My smile was lasting longer and longer. The interesting thing was that I really started trying harder. I was looking at my crown impressions and wondered what the endodontist would think. I was spending a few extra minutes putting more anatomy in my fillings to make them look more real. I was being a little pickier on the shade selections of my cosmetic cases. I was double checking the uncut dies to see if there was anything I could improve upon. In short, those simple compliments made me want to live up to them.

Bear with me for a short interlude.

I belong to a disability doctors' group. We have thirteen total dentists that meet twice a year. If one of us is out of commission for any length of time, our chairman (for the year) assigns us days to go into the affected dentist's office and work for free that day. Since we all work four-day weeks, if one dentist is down, we have twelve days left to work, which means we work one day outside of our own office every three weeks until the dentist gets better. It's a beneficial plan for all of us. The injured or ill dentist gets to keep up a revenue stream (even if it's a little limited) and we all know if we fall, we will be picked up. We've had to save each other a few times and it has worked out very well.

It was time for one of our biannual group meetings, which we hold on a rotational basis (alphabetically) at each doctor's office. The host caters dinner, which is usually salad, pizza, beer, soft drinks, and water. Sometimes we even get dessert. The actual meeting takes about two to three minutes while we all check in. Then we gossip and talk about our dental world. Occasionally, someone will suggest a "pearls" meeting, during which we all present our favorite instrument, restorative technique/material, marketing ideas, etc. So, what does this have to do with the compliments from my endodontist?

One of the newer dentists to the group wanted us to hear about his discovery of an endodontist to whom he just started sending cases. It was the same one I had been using. "This guy is great," said Dr. Newbee. "Not only do his finished endo's look absolutely perfect, but he also makes a point of complimenting me to all of his patients."

I kept my face as straight as I could, but I think my cheeks might have flushed just a bit. After I got over my snit, I realized how brilliant this endodontist's marketing was. He found something nice to say about every referring dentist to every patient he saw. It not only made the patient feel very good about their choice of dentist, but also made the dentist want to send more cases specifically to him. Brilliant! Now, how could I use that in my practice?

I realized that there were at least two things I could do. The first was when I examined a new patient and we charted every tooth, I always found at least one tooth that was "superbly treated." I would exaggerate how skilled the dentist was (but only a little) and mention that I might call the dentist later to give some positive reinforcement (we discussed this briefly in Chapter Nine). Did the patient remember who did that specific restoration? If they knew who it was, I would get the info to definitely make the call and then report back to the patient at a later visit. This made the patient feel good. And don't forget one of our mantras, "People won't remember what you said or did, but they will remember how you made them feel." So, patients will remember when we made them feel good. And they will also see us as a positive dentist who always sees the good side of dentistry.

The second thing I did was call all of my favorite specialists and ask each of them (separately) to lunch (my treat). I explained what had happened with the endodontist. I told them that because of the compliment, I really wanted to improve. I also told them how I found out that this was his normal modus operandi with all his referring dentists and how I really was only special in my own mind. I then asked my lunch guest to do the same. "Please find something that you can compliment exuberantly about my dentistry. It can be anything from tooth shade selection, diagnosis, eye for detail, or even my very competent staff." The key was to be positive about me, to let the patient know that the specialist knew me, worked with me, and enjoyed seeing my patients because I was 'that' good. It didn't matter what about me was good, just that it was said. And of course, they all agreed.

With a few of my specialists it took more than one lunch, but they all got the idea before long. The specialist that said something nice about me to the patient naturally got more referrals. In the beginning, I wrote a thank you note to all of them if I heard something back from the patient. It was usually in the form of an afterthought. "Dear Dr. Yankenpull: I just wanted to write you a quick note about Dorothy Sauerapple. She thought you did an outstanding job of placing the implant. She had had no pain and thought you were very gentle. She also liked your staff. **And she told me that you really thought I was a great dentist**. Thank you for that. I think we have a fully happy and grateful patient." If I had the email address, then the note went directly to the front office so that the entire office would know. Even though this marketing idea is a little self-serving, it really does work. You will have an easier time with your case acceptance, and your patients will have an easier time referring new patients to you.

"You really should see Dr. Disraeli. He's really top-notch. When I went to get a root canal, the specialist couldn't stop talking about how good he was."

I have incorporated this positive energy so that now it feels very natural to me. One day I was removing an onlay from a patient with the intention of replacing it. She had been with me for about five years and was fairly comfortable in my chair. The original onlay was chipped just enough to warrant making a new one. As I was removing the old restoration, I was astounded by how well the fit and color made it difficult for me to find the margins. I told the patient how incredible the original onlay was. I went on for a bit and perhaps a little too long. Her response was garbled because I had placed a rubber dam on her, so I asked yes or no questions. I told her that if she knew who the dentist was, I was going to call and brighten their day. Did she know who it was? She did and she tried to say something else, but it was too incomprehensible, and she finally gave up.

When I removed the dam, the first thing she said was the name of the dentist, "It's your friend Andy from L.A. He referred me to you five years ago." I smiled and decided to write him an email via his front office that afternoon. I told him the full story. I got a phone call that night from Andy. He told me that I had made his day, his year, and his career. He was very happy. And so was I.

I Want a High-End Hygienist.
Wait, What is a High-End Hygienist?

CHAPTER EIGHTEEN

Over the years I've seen a lot of hygienists, and they have all been different. Some have been pretty bad and didn't last long, and others have been superb and lasted quite a while. The bad ones can decimate your practice and the opposite is true of the excellent ones. So, what is the difference?

A hygiene school moved to my city and my favorite dental assistant, Lola, applied and got in. My loss, her gain. Lola was in her early thirties and was an employee with initiative. She always wanted to push the bounds of her license by asking to do things that weren't quite legal, even though she knew what my answer would always be. Her sense of humor was a bit on the snarky but fun side. When she found a product that was highly rated and less expensive, she always brought it to my attention when the supply reps came in. She kept the supply inventory up to date and neatly stocked. She was fun and very engaging with her patients. Her actual chairside skills were wonderful, and I really didn't want to have to lose her.

When she graduated hygiene school, she asked me for a job. Unfortunately, I didn't have any openings. She asked me to help her with interviews, and I said I would. I didn't want to tell her, "Just do your best. You're awesome and anyone can see that," because I felt that would have been lazy. I wrote some things down and spent some time with her. Then I realized that this could develop a good framework for a dentist hiring a hygienist that would help the practice. Here Is my best recollection of our conversation.

"Lola, why did you want to become a hygienist?" I asked. "And now that you've gone through school, do you still feel the same way about being a hygienist?" Her answer was brutally honest.

"I wanted to make more money." It was a simple answer and one that I realized was probably true of quite a few new hygienists. Earning a living for the money without really enjoying your career is very hard work. Was it my job to tell her what was great about hygiene? Maybe she would come to that conclusion on her own. I had a teaching moment. What fun.

"Oh, and by the way, never say money was your motivator in an interview." I strongly suggested. And then I asked her, "What are the costs involved with hygiene? In other words, how much money does the dentist make on each prophy?"

She guessed that the profit was probably about $25 to $50. I laughed. "An average cleaning is around $100 (at the time of this writing) and lasts an hour (forty-five to fifty minutes, allowing for room turnover). Salary is close to $50 per hour for an experienced hygienist. Payroll taxes, personal protective equipment, lights, disposables and giveaways, health and workers comp benefits, vacation, and sick pay eat up a good chunk of that. And let's not forget last minute cancelations and no-shows (one every other day is common in an average office), which is another chunk. Total for all expenses is…$90. A *$10 profit per cleaning*."

The numbers vary a bit between dental offices, but this gets the point across. The lesson to learn here is that the dentist makes money on the other things that a hygienist can offer. Whenever the prophy is the only procedure, the dentist basically breaks even. Hygienists have to understand this down to their core. Every dollar the patient spends beyond the prophy and in the same hour is pure profit. Dentists aren't greedy, but they're not offering hygiene for the fun of it. An exam by the dentist is $20-$100 (some dentists really *are* greedy). Arestin placement (*after* the cost of the Arestin) is about $20. Desensitization can be $20 to $50. Fluoride placement can be about $20 (or more). And don't forget about diagnosing (okay, actually "noticing") dentistry for the doctor to treat in the future."

I explained all this to Lola, and then I added, "This will take a break-even procedure into much higher numbers and make you a very valuable member of the team. But don't add anything that isn't indicated. Don't do unnecessary work—that pathway is a very slippery slope to sleepless nights."

She nodded in agreement.

"I'm telling you this so you can Inform the dentist who interviews you that you know how the process works," I explained. "Every little thing you add above and beyond a simple prophy improves the bottom line. Once you realize this, you become a very valuable member of the team. This is one of the reasons we are talking. What can you do? Everything! "

"Like what?" Lola asked.

"The minimum is to determine how often and what kinds of x-rays your doctor wants. How often does the doctor want exams to be done? Isn't it the job of the person scheduling to figure this out and let the hygienist know?" I asked rhetorically. "Absolutely," I answered without waiting, "but you are part of the team, and so far, everyone is human, so check, double check, and triple check when a patient comes in for a cleaning. What happens if you miss an exam or miss taking x-rays? Most of the time pretty much nothing, but should you take that chance on a patient with Sjogren's Syndrome, for example, or on an elderly patient who takes mouth-drying medications, or on that cancer survivor who had radiation on his salivary glands? You want your interviewing doctor to know that you pay attention to details."

"What kind of details?" she inquired, taking notes.

"Do a cancer check on every patient, for example. The chances that you will spy an actual cancer are maybe one in 50,000, but you still do it diligently on every patient, because you *are* diligent. I don't charge for cancer checks, but there are some incredible diagnostic tools available, and the dentists that have them rightfully charge for their use. Is it worth an extra $20 to you to make sure you get to keep all of your tongue? It's probably worth it to your patients. It's your job to make sure the patient doesn't feel like you are trying to charge them for every breath they take, but rather that they feel extremely well taken care of." I finished, finally taking a breath.

"I don't like to sell things. I just want to clean teeth and make some money" she declared truthfully.

"If that's the way you feel, you are going to end up in a job punching a timeclock with other minimally paid co-workers. They won't help you, they won't encourage you, and they probably won't be your friends. I've known you for several years and that's not you." I tried to discourage her from accepting that hourly-wage mentality.

"Lola, in your new position you need to be a salesperson. It doesn't have to be hard-core, slick-back-your-greasy-hair sales, but it is important to know that you are part of the team. You need to understand your role on that team. For example, a two-party sale is when one person recommends something, and another person independently says the same thing, thereby enhancing the value of the sale. When you, as a hygienist, tell a patient that there is something suspicious under the margin of a crown and point this out to your doctor in front of the patient, it becomes much easier for the doctor to diagnose and for the patient to accept the *needed* dentistry. The patient might have some skepticism if the doctor pointed something out after the hygienist just spent the last hour with the patient and didn't *notice* or say anything. Regardless, if the patient feels they're paying for the dentist's kids' college fund just by being in that exam room, they do trust the hygienist." At this point, I thought I was getting through to her.

"Find out what your doctor is comfortable with regarding root planing and curettage, sealants (does the hygienist place them, and if so, do you get an hour), antibiotic placement, adult and child fluoride placement, mouthwashes like peridex, etc. Find out if your doctor does (and enjoys) cosmetic dentistry, orthodontics, TMJ, sleep apnea, implants (placing and restoring), crowns and bridges, root canals, extractions, periodontal surgery, etc." I really wanted Lola to understand this and make sure she addressed it in her interview.

"As you know, in my office the hygienists look for cracks in teeth and know the difference between a surface crack (like a craze line) and something deeper. They look for worn incisal edges, open margins, and in short, anything out of the ordinary.

The more comfortable you are with this, the more confident you will be. And the more confident you are, the more valuable you will be to the dentist." Phew, that was a lot.

"Yes," she said tentatively. "I do see what you're saying."

"Lola, this next part is so important," I continued. "Every time your doctor does an exam on one of your patients, have at least one thing to tell your doctor to concentrate on IN FRONT OF THE PATIENT. This is probably the most important thing I can tell you. If you can fully embrace this concept, you will be extremely valuable."

"But then aren't I over-diagnosing?" she asked?

"No! You're creating a win-win situation. Because even if the doctor doesn't see a problem, the dentist will say, 'Let's keep an eye on this,' and then follow up with a compliment to you for being eagle eyed. If this is not part of your doctor's habit, then strongly suggest it. Compliments to a staff member ALWAYS make the doctor look good. On the other hand, if there is a problem, then the patient gets an early fix, you get another compliment, and the doctor gets some production. In both situations, the patient feels you are careful and diligent. If your doctor *doesn't* handle this correctly, you can be made to look like a greedy, commission oriented, money-grubbing pig. However, if handled correctly, the patient's experience and trust is enhanced."

She laughed at the money-grubbing pig comment.

"If you recognize problems that your doctor does not like to treat or if you're suggesting treatment that is different from what your doctor likes to do, then things might get a little dicey. In that case, it's better to recognize the problem only and then write it down since your doctor has inhaled way too many mercury fumes to recall your conversation of thirty seconds prior. Actually, there is something about having it written on paper that makes it more legitimate and believable. It definitely adds weight and credibility... gravitas. The important thing is that you are helping the patient get what needs to be done and your doctor begins to trust you more."

Lola nodded more confidently.

"Now let's talk about actually treating a patient. The rule is to always give positive reinforcement. People will not remember what you said to them a year later, but they will remember how you made them feel."

"Yes, I know. You say that all day long!" Lola good-naturedly complained.

"From the first moment a patient walks in, make it a good memory. Think about a patient who hasn't had his teeth cleaned in several years. The chances are that he is embarrassed by the lapse. The worst thing you could do is imply by gesture, posture, frown, or actually say something that reinforces his embarrassment. Is it honestly your goal to make this person feel worse? Because if you do, even unintentionally, then another five years will go by in between cleanings, since he did not have a great experience. When I look at a health/dental history and see that it has been longer than normal since the last dental visit, the first thing I do is smile and say, 'Welcome back to dentistry. We are all glad you are here.' At no time do I make the patient feel bad about poor brushing or a lack of flossing. I always turn it around and give positive feedback. I'll say something like 'You are doing very well brushing these front teeth. They look very clean. But it looks like you are having a harder time getting the back teeth. May I show you some techniques to make it easier?' or 'We find that most patients don't floss every day because they never get into the habit. They usually floss for a few days before the appointment and then when their teeth are clean, they relax. Why don't you try maintaining your newly clean teeth for thirty days after your prophy to see if you can get in the habit? It usually works wonders.' As opposed to, 'You know if you flossed more, this visit would be a lot easier on you!'

Lola laughed at the bluntness of my last comment.

"If you want to be the hygienist that patients request, make them feel good. If you want to stand out in your office, make the doctor feel good," I concluded. "Do you think you can get these points across to your interviewing dentist?" I asked.

"I think so," Lola replied, a little worried.

"Good." I paused for effect. "And there's more." I added.

Lola smiled and tried hard not to roll her eyes.

"Pain is a topic that's pretty self-evident. Don't hurt your patients! Even if you cure their periodontal disease, a year from now, they'll remember the pain."

"I know," said Lola. "You say that all the time, too. *I remember.*"

I reminded her again anyway. "Whenever I see a new patient who hasn't been seen in over a year (and after I welcome them back to dentistry and chat for a few minutes), I warn them that it may take more than one visit to get them clean. I remind them of what they learned in fifth grade about plaque and that if left long enough it gets a little too hard to remove with a toothbrush. Hopefully, at this point, they won't question a second visit cleaning fee. If I do a bad job of this, then the only thing the patient hears is that it will cost twice as much as their last cleaning with that guy down the street."

"Got it," she replied to my unasked question.

"The important thing for the hygienist, while working on this patient, is to pick up on the non-verbal cues. Did you see an eye close halfway during an injection? A louder than normal intake of breath? The proverbial white knuckle? Or the very blatant, 'You're horrible at this,' comment?

She laughed. "I hope no one would say that to me!"

"Okay, this next bit of advice can be fairly long, so I'll just sum it up. Let the interviewer know that you like to get to know your patients."

Lola looked a little overloaded and seemed to appreciate the abbreviation. "This I already understand," she said.

"When you get to know the patients, they become connected to another person in the office, and then they feel *even more* connected to the office overall."

"The added bonus is that I might make some friends," she said with a smile.

"Wow, you got it right in one," I said with encouragement.

"I cheated," laughed Lola. "You told me this when you first trained me," Lola laughed.

"All right! Then let's sum it all up. During your interview be prepared to let the dentist know you understand that dentistry is a business." And then I had her write down the following list:

1. Understand how two-party sales work.

2. Always have something for the dentist to look at during the exam.

3. Double check the treatment plans and the timing on x-rays and exams.

4. Always compliment the patient and reinforce positive traits.

5. Always find something nice to say in front of the patient about the dentistry of your dentist.

6. Be thorough but not painful.

"And above all, just do your best. You're awesome and anyone can see that." I concluded.

She left much more enlightened about her new career as a hygienist, if not a little overwhelmed about her role on the dental office team.

And if you are the dentist interviewing a new hygienist for your office, listen during the interview to see if you can discern any of the above points. This advice is not just for new hygienists like Lola, but It's also for doctors like you, looking to build the best staff possible for a long and happy career.

Lola had troubles with her first interview, but she decided it wasn't the type of office she wanted. The introductions to the staff during an office tour revealed a group of people who didn't really like each other. She didn't want to become one of them. She told me she looked at her notes about what we had discussed and nailed the next interview. She said it was a lot like our office without all the sayings, mottos, and quotes. Then she winked at me.

Patient Financial Plan?
Who Needs a Financial Plan?
I Do! I Do!

CHAPTER NINETEEN

Things were once again going well in the practice, and yet I felt tense knowing I was due for another disaster. I was far enough into my career to know that there was always something coming around the corner that I had either not anticipated or had forgotten to set up earlier (more often the latter). There were always more things I could do with my team. For example, I always wanted to write a manual about everything in the office, but that seemed so boring and a little pointless since we changed things so frequently. Ah, the ignorance, stupidity and laziness of youth.

My accounts receivable (AR) were a little higher than I wanted. I heard in a seminar that the AR should be about 1.5 times the monthly gross production, so I wanted to be as close to that as I could. To be fair, I changed that metric a few years later with a little help from my peers. Several of them bragged that they had no AR above and beyond the waiting insurance checks. Another said he didn't even bill insurance but gave his patients superbills if they wanted their insurance to pay. I wasn't there yet. I knew there were practices out there that could do that, but I really didn't think my patient population could go completely in that direction. I had attended seminars that encouraged us to go there, but that hill was a little too steep for me.

But back to my uneasiness. I was putting money away in savings for college funds for my three sons and for my retirement. As a result, I wasn't living too frivolously. After talking to my friends about AR, I decided to dive a little deeper. I thought about what the real numbers should be, so I pulled up the latest AR report to see how close I truly was.

When you look at the numbers in an AR report, they are divided out by 0-30, 30-60, 60-90, and over 90 days. There is also a division for insurance income and a last column for total AR. The total AR was the number I wanted (about 1.6X production at the time), but I realized that the majority of the amount due was in the "over 90-day column." I did some more analysis, this time looking at the individual accounts. There were patients who hadn't paid anything in six months and were still getting statements that I'm sure immediately went into the trash. There were patients who were paying $10 a month on a $5,000 account. There was a lot of irresponsible accounting, and I realized I had let things slip.

Then the following comment came from a patient to me *in person*, after the delivery of a crown:

"Dr. Disraeli, you never told me the cost of this crown. I can't afford $1,500. I just assumed it would be the same cost as the last one, and I even have a check for $795 right here." Then he brandished a signed check at me. He threw it down and marched out the door. "You can sue me for the rest," he yelled, as he slammed the door with a roomful of waiting patients looking on.

"But…" I stammered, "The last crown we did was 18 years ago."

Obviously, no one had spoken to him about the costs involved. I pulled in the entire office for a meeting to discuss an action plan. We worked out a system that we would follow for every patient that needed treatment on everything other than a standard prophy, and even then, there were some patients that needed the financial plan.

The system was very simple: Every patient would have a conversation with a financial consultant (office manager, receptionist, scheduler, dental assistant, etc.). During that time, the patients would be asked:

1. Were there any questions about the procedure(s)?

2. Did you understand the risks, benefits, and approximate costs of other alternatives?

3. Did you understand what would happen if you did nothing?

At this point, you present the fees for the diagnosed procedures. In my office, we also offer a discount if they pay on the same day the procedure is started. The total fee is reduced by ten percent, and therefore, their portion is also reduced. If they ask for alternatives, we say that you can pay half on preparation of crowns and half on delivery with no discount, but there are no options for fillings, etc.

The hard part is when patients go back on their word.

"Mr. Fatlier," Jane, my office manager started.

"You can call me Big, little darlin," the patient interrupted.

"Well, Big, with your same-day discount, as you know, your portion today is $942.83. Your insurance will pay the rest. It's the same amount that one of your coworkers had, so I'm fairly confident about the amount. Will that be check or credit card?" Jane smiled. She knew not to say anything else.

"I just wanted to let you know that it's raining today in Seattle, and I'll pay you next Tuesday," Big explained.

"Huh…what?" Jane stammered.

"The rain is my excuse. It really doesn't matter what the *actual* excuse is, it's just an excuse."

Needless to say, we all get patients who don't pay what they promised, so what do you do? Our plan was to make sure we contacted the patient on a scheduled basis with a scripted message. Obviously, they would get more severe with each subsequent message, but they would never cross over to be inappropriate or unprofessional. As a joke, the office had a lot of fun with silly over-the-top ideas (that we'd never do), like hiring a detective to follow delinquent patients around and get dirt that we could secretly publish. Or "roofie" a patient who blatantly refused to pay for services rendered (even though they were pleased with the work), and then take scandalous photos that we would send to his wife. These ridiculous, hypothetical scenarios were just our way of blowing off steam regarding unscrupulous patients who blatantly took advantage of our services.

The first messages would be more like reminders; after all, we did want Big to come back for more treatment. But after we realized that he was not answering our requests for payment, we would get a bit more severe. The final three notices would basically be a statement of "we're giving up on you returning to our office, but you still have to pay." The first of these final three would sorrowfully announce that we will need to take legal action if this is not dealt with promptly, the second gives a timeline, and the third says that we have turned over the account to a collection agency. If at any time the patient calls and is contrite, we will try to work with them. When they say they need time, I have found that the best way is to get a credit card number and an amount they are comfortable with and charge it every month until the account has zeroed out. If this patient needs more treatment, the only way you'll deal with them is to get the credit card number before the first procedure has begun. Run the card and make sure it goes through.

Work with your team to figure out the timing of your letters and make sure you follow up on all of your plans. After using this system over a three-year period, our AR went from 1.5X of our monthly production to .25X.

Do you need a written financial plan for every patient? Absolutely! You have too many patients with too many scenarios to keep track of individual needs. Work on writing up your own universal iron-clad formula and use it. Get your staff to use it on every patient where insurance isn't at full coverage. If there is someone special that you want to treat with financial kindness, you can easily make an exception, but the default should be in place for every patient.

The Finale...Almost

CHAPTER TWENTY

There is a lot of information in the previous chapters and there really is quite a bit more regarding the business of dentistry. Treat my story as a manual for your practice. Read a chapter at a time and gradually weave it into your practice. Too much, too soon will be frustrating, but slow learning will be rewarding. Give yourself permission not to hurry.

There are many ways to continue to learn, including weekend seminars, dental business management services (usually a one-year minimum commitment and very expensive), books, and study clubs. But you have to do something to improve (and keep improving) your practice. You can't stick your head in the sand and expect everything to always go well. As you can see in my dental career, I tried that and failed again and again.

But I succeeded as well.

Of course, success, like beauty, is in the eyes of the beholder. For me, success was:

1. Having patients who were happy with both their results and the process.

2. The ability to be happy doing actual dentistry and constantly improving my technique.

3. To know that my work will last.

4. Having the time to get to know a lot of people and creating long term relationships with many of them.

5. Learning from my mistakes.

6. Being able to mentor new dentists and hygienists.

7. Earning a living wage with enough to fund both my retirement and my sons' education.

In my career, I have watched many new dentists go to work for DMO's (Dental Maintenance Organizations). These are very large corporations that have fine-tuned the business of dentistry in a very strict, step-by-step process. Even the language is controlled. They are successful and they not only make a lot of money for themselves, but they also make a lot of money for the dentists. The problems are:

1. Due to overdiagnosis, patients go into debt.

2. Dentists often treat beyond their skill levels, and...

3. ...dentists don't have enough time for the procedures they know well.

4. Patients are rushed into signing contracts before they fully understand what they're signing.

It's all very legal but stretches the limits of ethics. Many young dentists leave the DMO world after becoming disillusioned and either buy or start their own practice, go into an associateship, or go back to school to specialize. However, many of the habits they learned in the first few years after dental school will remain.

The good news is that these dentists are searching for something better. This book is dedicated to them.

Thank you for reading it.

Bonus!
Thirty Quick Ideas that You Should Do Slowly

CHAPTER TWENTY-ONE

My friend, Andy (the Beverly Hills dentist), and I would meet frequently, and as much as we would try to avoid it, we would always discuss dentistry. We would bounce ideas off each other and then try various concepts and improvements in our offices to become better businesspeople. We both realized that if we tried to implement too many ideas at once, nothing would be get done. Each new concept needed its own space to fully mature, and we needed acceptance from the rest of the team. The following are some of the ideas we came up with. If you decide to try out some or all of these, make sure you perfect each one before moving on. We thought we were very innovative and special. Most of these were not *that* innovative, but that didn't diminish their importance.

So here we go.

1. **Use Intra-Oral photography:** This is one of my favorite tools. There are so many on the market that it gets a little confusing. Make sure the picture quality is crisp and clean. Make sure that the system works seamlessly with your dental software. And play with it a little to feel comfortable with the way it handles. Intra-oral photography gives instant validation to your diagnosis. Your patient sees what you see.

"You need a crown," said Dr. Slick convincingly.

"My tooth feels fine," said Thomas Doubter, unconvinced.

"Let's get a close-up of that tooth." Dr. Slick took a photo, placed it on the large monitor facing Thomas, and explained what he was seeing. "That orange-ish brown color next to the giant silver filling is decay. Please note that it is a lot of decay. In fact, I'm not sure that we aren't already looking at a root canal."

"Can we start this afternoon?" begged Thomas Doubter.

Intra-oral photography works because your patient no longer has to take your descriptive word at face value. Now they can see for themselves. Once you explain what a tooth is supposed to look like and show them that it doesn't look like that, your three steps of adding value become more believable.

2. **Apply quadrant dentistry:** Can you do three crowns in maybe twenty-five percent more time than doing one? Or four fillings instead of two? How much time do we waste cleaning, anesthetizing, chatting, cleaning up? You'll be making so much more money that you can afford to discount it a little as an inducement to doing it all at once. When you take pre-op photos for a cosmetic case that was originally planned for six teeth, but you notice that the first bicuspids are very visible and very ugly, how much would it really cost you to do one at no charge if your patient will pay for the other one? Another example would be when you have a legitimate reason for retreating three of four fillings in one quadrant, but the fourth one will probably need to be done within a few years. You won't run behind adding one more tooth to treat. Why not do it at no cost and give your patient another reason to stay with you? If they are extremely grateful, ask for a testimonial, review, or recommendation to a friend.

3. **Apply metrics to see where you have been:** Metrics will tell you how many crowns you average per month. It will tell you what the average worth of a new patient will be. It will give you information on the success rate of your treatment planning. Are you on an upward or downward trajectory?

Below is a useful model. If you know you'll never do this, skip to the next idea (because this one is not quite quick), but a picture tells a thousand words. Use the following Excel chart in Figure 1 as a guide. Plug in the procedures and activities you wish to follow. This first graph is a yearly accumulation of data broken into columns and rows by month. The last columns give totals of the previous twelve months, and the last column gives a monthly average.

	JAN	FEB	MAR	APR	MAY	JUNE	JULY	AUG	SEP	OCT	NOV	DEC	TOTAL	MONTHS	AVERAGE
PROD*													0	0	#DIV/0!
COLL*	#DIV/0!	#DIV/0!	#DIV/0!	#DIV/0!	#DIV/0!	#DIV/0!	#DIV/0!	#DIV/0!	#DIV/0!	#DIV/0!	#DIV/0!	#DIV/0!	#DIV/0!	0	#DIV/0!
PROD/DAY	#DIV/0!	#DIV/0!	#DIV/0!	#DIV/0!	#DIV/0!	#DIV/0!	#DIV/0!	#DIV/0!	#DIV/0!	#DIV/0!	#DIV/0!	#DIV/0!	#DIV/0!	0	#DIV/0!
NP*													0	0	#DIV/0!
AR*													0	0	#DIV/0!
0-30*													0	0	#DIV/0!
30-60*													0	0	#DIV/0!
60-90*													0	0	#DIV/0!
>90*													0	0	#DIV/0!
EIP*													0	0	#DIV/0!
#DAYS*													0	0	#DIV/0!
POSS HYG*													0	0	#DIV/0!
ACTL HYG*													0	0	#DIV/0!
UTILIZATION	#DIV/0!	#DIV/0!	#DIV/0!	#DIV/0!	#DIV/0!	#DIV/0!	#DIV/0!	#DIV/0!	#DIV/0!	#DIV/0!	#DIV/0!	#DIV/0!	#DIV/0!	0.00%	#DIV/0!
PT./DAY	#DIV/0!	#DIV/0!	#DIV/0!	#DIV/0!	#DIV/0!	#DIV/0!	#DIV/0!	#DIV/0!	#DIV/0!	#DIV/0!	#DIV/0!	#DIV/0!	#DIV/0!	0.00	#DIV/0!
HYG$/MO*	#DIV/0!	#DIV/0!	#DIV/0!	#DIV/0!	#DIV/0!	#DIV/0!	#DIV/0!	#DIV/0!	#DIV/0!	#DIV/0!	#DIV/0!	#DIV/0!	0.00	0	#DIV/0!
HYG$/DAY	#DIV/0!	#DIV/0!	#DIV/0!	#DIV/0!	#DIV/0!	#DIV/0!	#DIV/0!	#DIV/0!	#DIV/0!	#DIV/0!	#DIV/0!	#DIV/0!	0.00	0	#DIV/0!
QUADS*	#DIV/0!	#DIV/0!	#DIV/0!	#DIV/0!	#DIV/0!	#DIV/0!	#DIV/0!	#DIV/0!	#DIV/0!	#DIV/0!	#DIV/0!	#DIV/0!	#DIV/0!	0	#DIV/0!
FILLS*													0	0	#DIV/0!
FILLS/DAY	#DIV/0!	#DIV/0!	#DIV/0!	#DIV/0!	#DIV/0!	#DIV/0!	#DIV/0!	#DIV/0!	#DIV/0!	#DIV/0!	#DIV/0!	#DIV/0!	0.00	0.00	#DIV/0!
CROWNS*													0	0	#DIV/0!
CRNS./DAY	#DIV/0!	#DIV/0!	#DIV/0!	#DIV/0!	#DIV/0!	#DIV/0!	#DIV/0!	#DIV/0!	#DIV/0!	#NAME?	#DIV/0!	#DIV/0!	#DIV/0!	0	#DIV/0!
FLUORIDE													0	0	
ARESTIN*													0	0	
MAGIC #*													0.00	0	#DIV/0!
B#AVE*													0	0	#DIV/0!
BONUS*													0	0	#DIV/0!
Pt. 12 Mo's*													0	0	#DIV/0!
Pt. 24 Mo's*													0	0	#DIV/0!
Pt. 36 Mo's*													0	0	#DIV/0!
TOTAL	0	0	0	0	0	0	0	0	0	0	0	0	0	11	0

Figure 1

Figure 2 is a monthly graph which follows new patients from the day they first come in:

A. Did you send them a welcome?

B. Did you send their referral source a thank-you note?

C. Write the total in dollars of the treatment plan.

D. Go back after one year and total the amount paid for that year.

E. At the end of the month, total up the treatment plan dollars.

F. At the end of the month, total up the actual dollars the patient spent.

G. Divide 'E' into 'F' and get the percentage effectiveness of your treatment.

DATE	NEW PATIENT	REFERRED BY	NP LETTER DONE	RF LETTER SENT	GIFT SENT	$ Dx DAY 1	MO $TOTAL	$ 1 YR Dx COMPLETED	$ 1 YR Dx COMPLETED TOTAL	% ACCEPTANCE

Figure 2

I did this second graph fifteen years ago and found out that my one-year percentage success rate was high. But there was a problem. At that time, I was a little lazy and hadn't done the one-year numbers in a few years. I had an assistant who liked to do this kind of data entry and when she had time, she put it together for me. Although the first year looked very good, the retention rate of the patients after completing their first year of treatment was depressingly low. I realized I had pumped a lot of energy into that first year and took it for granted that the patients would stay with me. We had an office meeting and came up with a way to let our patients know we appreciated them, which leads to the next quick idea.

4. **Write "bun" letters:** These are letters we write to patients who have been with us for over a year (and many who have been with us for over a decade). It is a letter that a staff member sends, thanking them for being a patient, commenting on something they talked about, or encouraging them in their dental world. We called it a bun letter because someone in the office said that when the patient opens and reads our note, it makes them feel the same way the aroma of a 'fresh out of the oven' roll smells. Something else happened when we started this project. A few of our staff with less outgoing personalities started engaging more with their patients in order to get something to write about.

5. **Create a marketing plan:** Do you have a marketing plan? What is a marketing plan? If you're like me, you just got a stomach-ache. My marketing plan used to be "treat patients well and they'll send their friends." That's not a plan, it's a motto. A marketing plan is the blueprint that a dental office will use to sell its services. It will tell you who your customers are, how to reach them effectively, and what cost point is just right. A marketing plan will also help you measure how well you are doing. Dentistry is very competitive and laziness in this area will be harmful to your growth. Find someone to help you, even if you have to go to the nearest college or university to find an upper classman who needs experience. Start with a web designer that fully understands search engine optimization (SEO).

6. **Understand internal versus external marketing:** When you have a marketing plan in place you will use both of these methods. External marketing is paying for ads to get new patients with no direct relationship to the office. Internal marketing uses existing patients and staff to help you. A real simple way to figure out if you are ready for external marketing is to imagine someone coming into your office for a first visit. This person just walked by and noticed that this dental office looked nice from the outside and called to make an

appointment. There were no referrals and no one to sing your praises. What are the chances that your team can convert this stranger into becoming a "forever" patient? Do you trust the person answering the phone to fully convince this person to believe in you? Will this person be impressed with your staff and the way you handle a first visit? What are the chances that you will be doing eighty to ninety percent of treatment that was diagnosed? (See the idea above on metrics.) If any of these answers are unfavorable, then why would you spend money trying to get some stranger to become a patient when the odds are that they probably won't even start their treatment plan? It will be a lot less expensive and much more cost effective once you get your internal systems in place. Don't waste money on external marketing until you're ready to exploit it to the max.

7. **Create a discount quick-call list:** Your regular quick-call list is your list of patients that you know (because you asked) who would like to come in earlier than their scheduled appointment. It might be because you are very busy or because their desired appointment was on a day that had no openings. They know that a call to come in earlier might not work for them, but they'd like to be asked, and it actually might work for them. Everybody wins.

   Your discount quick-call list is a list of those patients that you know are having trouble with the cost of dentistry (because they told you). It would be very easy to ask them if they would like to be called if a short-notice opening occurred, and as a reward for filling our gap, they could receive a discount. I have offered up to fifty percent off the amount they would have to pay out of pocket. We know that insurance only pays half of a crown. If the patient has insurance, the discount would only be twenty-five percent of the entire fee (and you would receive seventy-five percent). If there is no insurance, then the discount would be the full fifty percent. The amount you discount isn't that important, but don't be a penny pincher. Today's schedule is the most important one, then the next day, etc. Every office has patients that need dentistry but are less than wealthy. A discount quick-call list has no downside. An empty chair still has overhead. Worry about tomorrow's empty chair after today's chair is filled. If you have a last-minute cancellation and you now have a two-hour opening, what can you do? (The crossword is beckoning, and that coffee won't drink itself, hmm.) Pull out your discount quick-call list.

8. **Read "The One Minute Manager" by Ken Blanchard:** It will take you a little longer than a minute, but given that none of us ever trained to be managers, this book is incredible at getting the best out of your team.

9. **Refund rapidly:** If you are doing a good job with collections, you will over-collect on some patients as insurance payments change for the better. Make it a point to refund these overpayments quickly. Try to get them in the mail (or electronic transfer if you are so inclined) before the patient realizes there is money owed. There is nothing more satisfying to your team than when a patient calls asking for overpayment money to be returned and the response is, "Check your mail today, Mrs. Diamond. It was sent out on Monday."

10. **Learn about Care Credit (and other types of medical debit cards):** This is a way for a patient to borrow money that is quick, easy, and cheap. The process is simple. It takes less than ten minutes to process and is done in your office once you have completed an initial setup. The concept is that the lender (Care Credit, et al) will give the borrower a debit card. A procedure is done, and **on the same day,** the borrower uses the debit card to pay their dental bill. The provider gets instant payment with an approximately ten percent reduction in the fee. The borrower has up to a year to pay the money back with no interest. The timeline of the "no-interest" loan is a contract between the provider and the lending company. The discount percentage is

a reflection of the timeline, so once the timeline is established, it is absolute. If the patient does not follow the monthly payments, they will pay a penalty, and it's usually stiff. The very good news about that missed payment is the dentist has no need to know because they already have their money. That "infidelity" is between the borrower and lender alone. Since I usually give a ten percent discount on same day payments (except PPO plans), this works very well for me. And clearly, if a patient uses Care Credit, I do not offer the discount. On the other side, credit cards will cost you one and a half to two and a half percent. If I offer the same ten percent in addition to the one and a half to two and a half percent, my total discount is now well over ten percent. Care Credit sounds pretty good for patients that need a little help, but if they are denied by Care Credit, why would *you* offer them credit? Care Credit takes all the risk.

11. **Communicate with your specialists:** This is so very important, and it needs to be in both directions. Don't forget that the specialist you use is a reflection on you. If they don't pump you up, if they have "heavy" hands, or if the patient's main contact is impatient, *you* will look bad. The only way you can deal with this is to find a better specialist. Conversely, if your specialist doesn't know why they're seeing your patient, who will the patient blame?

Let's start with your instructions to the specialist. Spend at least a few minutes introducing the patient and giving a little personal history. Give as much dental history as possible. Write down what you anticipate and what you want the specialist to do. Sometimes it really is as simple as asking for a full mouth periodontal evaluation. Or it's a little more precise when asking the endodontist to evaluate the crack on the distal wall of tooth number nineteen. Your instructions must beat the patient to the specialist's office. When the specialist speaks to the patient with knowledge, not only do you and the specialist look good, but the specialist opens up a more comfortable communication to help the patient.

On the flip side, the after-visit communication must get to you within two days (one day is better). Specialists like to give very thorough reports, but I want speed first and thorough later. The patients often call you to ask a post operative question about their treatment. They rightly assume that you have knowledge of everything that happened and can clarify their worries and instructions. (There have been times that I didn't know the answers, but I always made the phone call to the specialist to find out.) There is a specialist that I really like personally, but I won't send him patients. His reports started coming in one to two months after treatment. All of my pleas to be timelier were listened to, apologized for, and eventually ignored. When our office called to request a report, their office was unorganized, and the reports were very slow to come.

Find the best specialists and work hard on the communication.

12. **Build and keep your reputation:** It takes years to build a reputation and moments to destroy it. Look at your dentistry as if some other dentists were judging you, because they eventually will. Endodontists and periodontists will get intimate with your work. Oral surgeons will evaluate an extracted tooth to check out the fit of your restorations. Other dentists will treat your patients as they move to different areas. If you are not using a CADCAM, check your models before every cementation and learn from them. I always ask my lab for an extra untrimmed die to study (and possibly trim if the crown doesn't seat well, to see if my impression was warped or if the lab scratched the die). If you're using CADCAM, be very critical of the scan and be proud enough to show your patient. As you get better and your reputation improves, you'll know you're on the right track when labs and specialists start to see you as their personal dentist.

13. **Solve your problems generously:** Always take the high road and think of what you, as a patient, would want if the roles were reversed. Yes, it's the "Golden Rule," and it's still a very good guide to action. Certainly the patient's point of view in a dispute has to be seriously considered. Nevertheless, I would bet that most of the time the dentist and dentistry were correct, but the dentist did not explain things properly, didn't set expectations well, or inundated the patient with so much information that there was no way for them to understand it all. When confronted with an unhappy patient, be empathetic and do not become defensive. If you need a moment to rein in your knee-jerk response, leave the room for a moment saying, "I need to check in with a patient for just a moment and then I'll be back here to spend as much time as we need to understand what's going on." Then catch your breath and realize that your patient has a valid complaint. You can be right or happy, but rarely both. Please choose happy. When a refund is in order, remember this one incident won't stop you from paying your student loan bill, and an argument will only make the patient angry. In this world of social media and reviews, an irate patient can go a long way in disrupting your life. If we look at it from the side that the patient is right, solve the problem beyond their expectations. Be fast with a refund or an offer to redo the treatment at no cost. If you were going to do this anyway, do it quickly. There is nothing that diffuses an issue faster than saying, "You're right." If there is a dispute, solve it beyond the patient's expectation and you will get a rainmaker for life.

14. **Use your lab to the fullest:** When your practice is in its earliest stages, you have more time than patients, so it's cheaper for you to do your own lab work. You probably enjoy it because you're probably very good at it. But you're not fast. Once you get busier with patients, you start using a commercial lab more frequently because when you add up the cost of your time, you realize it's cheaper to send out the lab work. You feel relieved with saving time, but some

of your cases that come back may not meet your high expectations. If you are a normal dentist, you get angry and frustrated, "How could they send this mangled mess to me. I don't have time for this." At this point, you start looking for another lab. What you really should do is start looking at what you are sending and what you are asking of your lab. Before you get angry, look at the impressions you've sent out. Look at the models coming back. Are they pristine? Are you proud of them? When you start working with a new lab (or even your old lab), ask them to be critical of your work. Ask them to give you advice on how to make their job easier and how to bring you more success. They don't get this request very often and they'll have a tendency to minimize your faults. Beg them to be honest because you really want to be the best dentist you can be. If you send them excellent models, they will send you excellent cases. Your patient gets an easy delivery. You save time not having to adjust the case. Your patient is happy. The lab is happy. How could you *not* be happy? Sometimes you need to take a little risk and perhaps be a little vulnerable to be better. An added bonus is your reputation as a "quality" dentist will improve.

15. **Always assume the best about your colleagues:** Try to recall that patient of yours whose final restoration was only adequate because of their huge tongue, their excessive saliva, or the fact they were being entirely uncooperative. Other dentists have the same problems. Be slower in your criticism. We have a tendency to be quick with our knowledge about how the last dentist screwed up. Did you know that the filling you're criticizing was placed twenty years ago? Or that the family dentist tried to have the patient choose a crown, but the patient could only afford a monstrously large filling that wouldn't last? When you tell a patient that their restoration is subpar, it sounds like you're saying that you're better. Does your patient really need to hear you brag about how much better you can fill their dental needs? We, as a dental family, do not need to sling mud at our

peers. It makes all of us look bad. Instead, when you see good dentistry, compliment the dentist to the patient, and if possible, call the dentist. How many of those phone calls have you received?

16. **Start taking before and after photos:** Even if you don't do full anterior cosmetic work, patients like to see invisible dentistry (no pun intended). Put together a book (check out *www.Shutterfly.com*) and make multiple copies. Place them in every operatory and out in your waiting room. If you have a good rapport with a specialist (and you absolutely should), offer a book to them as well. When you start taking photos, you'll see things that weren't obvious to you before—things you were not proud of but looked okay under normal vision. You'll probably throw away a lot of photos in the beginning, but your quality of work will improve. Use a nice camera and learn how to use it. At every dental convention you can find a booth displaying high quality cameras with macro lenses using a color accurate flash. You can get photos from your iPhone, but it's difficult to get the depth of field needed for the photos you want.

17. **Own your dentistry:** I have an unwritten warranty on my dentistry. My entire team knows this and automatically enforces it. If a patient breaks a crown (or any restoration) within five years after I placed it, the new one will be at no charge to the patient, and I will apologize profusely for the inconvenience. I always ask how it broke, but I rarely get the truth. It doesn't matter, I'll redo it anyway. Patients *like* that you stand behind your dentistry. I believe it is illegal to guarantee your work in my state, but I also believe it is unethical to do poor dentistry. By having the unofficial, unwritten warranty, I hold my own feet to the fire to do the best dentistry I can. If you're thinking, "Hmm, the patient didn't brush their teeth or come in for regular appointments, why should you do free dentistry?" then you would have a point. Perhaps you didn't educate them on the perils of soda, or the pitfalls of a dry mouth. Did your office schedule them for a

visit and they didn't show up, or did your office fail to appoint them? How often does your dentistry fail within five years? Can you afford to do the very occasional restoration at no charge? Your patients will appreciate you and will definitely refer their friends.

18. **Offer holiday scholarships:** Every now and then, we have a patient who has needed to make payments due to unforeseen circumstances in their life. They have dutifully made their $25-to-$50 payment every month, but they're still several years away from getting out of dental debt. Right around the winter holidays, I ask my team to nominate a few deserving patients. We talk about them at meetings, and they argue for their choice. I pick a few and write off up to $500 per patient. We send a letter and usually get a huge thank you, and we always get a new patient within a year from our scholarship patient.

19. **Be on time:** Do you expect your patients to be on time? The excuse that you had an emergency causing you to be late works for that patient perhaps once every few years. People don't like to be kept waiting. Figure this out. How much time does it take for you to do a one surface filling? (And don't forget to add in the necessary conversation to put your patient at ease.) How about a crown preparation? How about a crown preparation on a lower second molar? Not all crowns are prepared equally, so why would you schedule them the same? How much time should we schedule for a root canal? Is it one canal or four? Have your assistant time you when you aren't paying attention to the clock. Have them time every procedure for a month (or longer). How much time do you need to be in the operatory? How much time does your assistant need? Evaluate and make changes so that you and your patients are on time. Patients love to brag about a dentist who is on time.

20. **Make your website professional:** What does your website say about you? Are you proud of it? A website is information about your office.

It needs to be easy to see and easy to navigate. At the very least, it is an invitation to come to your office and see you. At its best, it will cause a browser to stop looking and contact your office. There are a lot of web designers that can help you create something clean, informative, and user-friendly, plus they can make it integrate well with your marketing plan. A professional designer can also help with your SEO. It is definitely not too expensive and is absolutely necessary. Please don't spend money on a cookie-cutter website. It looks cheap and gives the impression that your dentistry is cheap as well.

21. **No pain:** Occasionally your injections will miss the nerve block, or the patient has an accessory nerve, but this should be rare. Your actual injection should be close to perfect and painless. On an upper arch (or a lower infiltration), inject for three seconds, remove the needle, and call that a comfort drop. Wait at least ten seconds and re-enter the same spot. Inject slowly. Ask the patient if they are feeling anything. If the answer is "no", then you've just reinforced your skill to the patient. On an inferior alveolar block, press the needle one to two millimeters in and inject for three seconds. I like to leave the needle in place and tell the patient in advance that this is what I will do, and then wait at least ten seconds. Push the needle in slowly to find your mark and give a one- to two-second injection again. Wait for ten more seconds and slowly deliver the rest of the carpule. It's always a good idea to ask the patient if they're okay or if they feel any discomfort. Don't start drilling too soon. Ask your patient if they have signs of numbness and anesthetize again if needed.

    Don't let a heavy-handed hygienist work in your office. Either try to train towards gentle, but thorough work, or say goodbye.

22. **Present a clean, attractive office to your patients:** Pretend you're a patient and walk into your office. What do you see? Is there a stain in the carpet or a smudge on the paint? Do the chairs in the waiting room look inviting and comfortable or do they look institutional?

What does it smell like? What do you hear? Do the operatories look neat, clean, and sterile? Do you have junk in a corner? Be critical and fix whatever bothers you.

23. **Keep patients' personal notes up to date:** There is a spot in every software that allows for personal notes that are tied to a specific patient. If you can't find it, contact your dental software representative and ask. I like to start this note with the date they first came in and their referral source. Then I enter their non-dental history like marital status, spouse's name, kids (with names and ages), occupation, pets, where they grew up, etc. Enter more if they are willing to share. There are two main reasons these notes are important. The first is that you engage the patient and, ultimately, as a result, you form a bond. The second is that your head is already filled to the max with the names and types of dental adhesives, remembering to put dental marketing in the front of your brain, the passwords to all of your streaming services, and more baby names than you thought possible. When you see the new patient who had no treatment needs six months later, can you remember anything about them? Simply go back to the notes and refresh your memory. If you were feeling lazy that day and only jotted down that they were a lawyer, then you have to pretend you remember them so that they don't feel like a wallet waiting payment. Have your team add something to these patient notes whenever possible. Marriages, births, deaths, large vacations, new jobs, etc. And you should refer to these notes occasionally as well. You might learn something.

24. **Give your patients five-star treatment:** Make your patients feel more special than the other dentists do. Give compliments to patients, hire and train good staff, and be efficient. Personalize their experience, be a good listener, call at night, be available, have staff walk all the way into the waiting room to introduce themselves, and greet them by name with a smile.

25. **Deal with your mistakes:** How else are we going to get better unless we recognize our mistakes and change what we need in order to make sure it doesn't happen again? When you see a mistake, write it down and deal with it later if at all possible. Give yourself time to think of a solution that works for everyone. Think about it and how to get the result you want. Firing from the hip is rarely good for all involved. You will probably see more of your own mistakes, and these are as important if not more so to manage. An extreme example might be a brief lapse when start drilling on the wrong tooth (or the wrong surface). You have a great assistant who pushes your drill out of the way with her suction tip, so the damage was only mental stress. What is the solution? Surgeons have started to place an "X" on the wrong side, but I don't think placing on "X" on all the other teeth is a logical solution. Instead, ask my assistant write on the paper where the surgical tray rests with pertinent information: Tooth number, surface, condition necessitating treatment, and age of old restoration. Another mistake might arise when you see a tooth next to the one you're working on that needs treatment as well. You raise the patient to a sitting position, explain the need, and they agree. Unfortunately you forget to check their insurance remaining. The first procedure emptied their reserves, and now you have to eat the cost. How do you solve this one? You have to remember to include your financial person in the discussion whenever there is a change. The only way to minimize the number of mistakes you make is to recognize them, solve them, and move on to the next situation.

26. **Compliment your patients:** I know, I know. I've said this multiple times already. Do you remember way back in the beginning of this book when we talked about mottos? People won't remember what you said or did, but they will remember how you made them feel. Compliment as often as possible! Compliment their previous dentist and compliment your staff in front of patients.

27. **Celebrate important dates:** How hard is it to keep track of the birthdays and anniversaries of your team members? Put it in your calendar and don't forget to add the spouses and children. Add the anniversary of their start date (working with you). Add the start date when they were licensed. Add when they are due for a review. Add any other important date and set a reminder for a few days in advance in case the 'event' warrants a bigger celebration. Your staff will brag about you, and you'll truly have an office family.

28. **Surprise your staff:** At least once a year I ask the scheduler to block off an entire day at least a month in advance. Then I ask them to fake a schedule with a lot of our least favorite patients. During the office meeting I wait for someone to realize it's going to be a bad day, and then I let everyone vent. I let it go on for a few moments, and then I stand up and say, "To hell with that! Let's cancel the day and play hooky!" Everyone laughs until they realize I'm serious. I then organize a carpool to go to a nice coffee shop—one that's not a national chain. When we get there and get the drinks we want (I pay for everything all day), I tell them of the plan for the next phase. I choose an event: something like going bowling, miniature golf, go-carting, etc. When we get there, I give them a timeline, and then we meet after the activity and go out for lunch at a nice restaurant. After lunch is another event like the first one, but in this case I add the possibility of a movie if the right one has just come out. It's easier getting tickets on a weekday afternoon than any evening or weekend. Another afternoon event is a trip to the mall. I have the staff pair up and I give them $200 each. My instructions are to buy something that is absolutely for yourself and there is a time limit. The team that gets closest to spending all the money before the time is up receives the change from the rest of the teams...and $50. I need receipts. By this time, it's getting close to the end of the workday. "Goodbye, and I'll see ya later."

29. **Deal with your red flags:** There are always a very small percentage of patients that make you groan when you see them on the schedule. These are the ones that put the exclamation point on the designation of a *red flag*. These are the patients who blame you for their problems. "I have perio disease and you haven't gotten me in to see your hygienist in over two years." Well, yes, we did try to reach out to you. We read you the list of the emails, texts, letters, and phone calls. You said you never received them.

> "I'm so sorry I missed my appointment last week. My grandmother died." Oh really. Isn't this the seventh time she died? Your excuse only works once or twice. Try to remember which professional you stood up next time.

> "Could you please recement that 6-unit bridge my last dentist made one more time?"

> "Oh my, I forgot my checkbook, credit cards, and my wallet. Ooh and guess what! We're going to Paris tomorrow, and I just can't think straight. Could you make this quick?"

> "I'm not nice and I never will be."

> "You keep raising your prices so that I can pay for your children's college tuition, room and board, and books. How do you like your new car that I paid for?" All I can say is thank you. Yep, I doubled my fee, but you never got the hint to try someplace cheaper.

I am giving you permission to remove these horrible people from your practice and give your team permission to nominate patients who are—at best—sucking your good will away. Have a team meeting and celebrate when you write that letter that your malpractice insurance company designates as acceptable. The letter basically says that you feel unable to meet the patient's dental needs. You will be available for the next sixty days for emergencies only (your insurance company knows the exact timing). If they need names of qualified dentists in their area, the local dental society has a list of licensed dentists. The number can be found on their website. Wish them well. The first time you do this it will feel wonderful. In fact, every time you do this it will feel wonderful.

30. **Do the right thing…always.**

Acknowledgements

Thank you to every dentist before me. From their mistakes and solutions, I have prospered. Thank you to everyone in my family who has read my scribbles and guided me, gently, into this book. And special thanks to Stacy Dymalski. You are truly the "Memoir Midwife."

About the Author

A medical professional by trade, and a storyteller at heart, Doug Disraeli, DDS, has deep roots in dentistry. The son and grandson of dentists, Dr. Disraeli grew up in San Diego and graduated dental school from the University of Southern California in 1982. After that, he returned to San Diego to continue the family legacy as a dentist. From there Dr. Disraeli began his journey in search of the secret to a thriving, ethical practice. By combining dentistry with good, old-fashioned kindness and respect for his patients and peers, Dr. Disraeli began curating his own collection of career golden nuggets that paved the way to a successful, lucrative practice of which he could be proud. Now, after thirty-plus years as a dentist, Dr. Disraeli shares his wealth of knowledge, so that new dentists may get a head start on their own successful careers. Married to his wife, Mindy since 1984, Dr. Disraeli has three grown sons (none of which are dentists) and enjoys hiking, sailing, and traveling with his family.

www.ingramcontent.com/pod-product-compliance
Lightning Source LLC
Chambersburg PA
CBHW031858200326
41597CB00012B/464